STUDIES IN NORTH-EASTERN

Religion, Business and Society in North-East England.
The Pease Family of Darlington
in the Nineteenth Century

STUDIES IN NORTH-EASTERN HISTORY

Series editor: Professor A. J. Pollard

1. *Symeon of Durham. Historian of Durham and the North*, ed. David Rollason (1998)

2. *The Battle of Neville's Cross 1346*, ed. David Rollason and Michael Prestwich (1998)

3. *Late Medieval Northallerton. A Small Market Town and its Hinterland, c.1470– 1540*, by Christine M. Newman (1999)

4. *Religion, Business and Society in North-East England. The Pease Family of Darlington in the Nineteenth Century*, by Anne Orde (2000)

Studies in North-Eastern History is a series published by Shaun Tyas for the North-East England History Institute, which is based on a confederation of the six north-east universities (Durham, Newcastle, Northumbria, Open University, Sunderland and Teesside), has links with local bodies and individuals in tourism, heritage, museums, libraries, historical and other groups in the community, and fosters research at the highest level through conferences, research groups and research projects on all aspects of North-East England's past.

STUDIES IN NORTH-EASTERN HISTORY

RELIGION, BUSINESS AND SOCIETY IN NORTH-EAST ENGLAND

The Pease Family of Darlington in the Nineteenth Century

ANNE ORDE

SHAUN TYAS

STAMFORD

2 0 0 0

.

Typeset from the disk of the author by the publisher

Published by

SHAUN TYAS
(an imprint of 'Paul Watkins')
18 Adelaide Street
Stamford
Lincolnshire, PE9 2EN.

ISBN

1 900289 40 7 (paperback)

1 900289 39 3 (hardback)

Printed and bound in the United Kingdom by the Alden Group, Oxford

CONTENTS

INTRODUCTION

In recent years there has been a renewal of interest in the relations between business and religion, going beyond discussion of theology on the one hand and Weberian models of the Protestant ethic on the other, and exploring the attitudes of actual Christian businessmen to wealth and success, the influence of religious belief on business practice, and so on. The present work may contribute to this discussion. It is an examination of one prominent Quaker family of industrialists, with a distinctive type of business, and their contribution to the economic, social and political development of North East England over the nineteenth century.

The fact of the Pease family's Quakerism was the subject of much comment in their day, and contemporaries tried to evaluate the influence that their particular religious affiliation had on their business conduct. There is therefore nothing especially new in approaching them from this angle. But it is possible now to look back over the evolution of English Quakerism and the English business class in a century of marked social and economic change, to draw some conclusions, and to examine in this context the ways in which members of this family promoted their distinctive business interests, used their wealth, and served their communities. The particular geographical context is of importance, since the Peases were among the initiators and promoters of the industrial development of North East England.

Business families in nineteenth-century Britain can on the whole be seen to conform to a general pattern, over several generations and across the denominational spectrum, of growing wealth, growing consumption, modification of puritan standards, and assimilation into a less business-oriented culture. To a considerable extent the way in which members of the Pease family handled their interests and chose their lifestyles fits the pattern. Closer examination of the lives of individuals, however, demonstrates the limitations of general statements. Not all Quaker business families and family businesses turned out the same way; not all differed markedly from other kinds of conscientious Nonconformist families or even Anglicans. And not all members of one family, even of the same generation, behaved alike or had the same attitude to their position. The Peases do not invalidate the general pattern; but they do enrich it with quite a range of variations.

The foundation of any modern work on the Pease family has to be the work of Professor Maurice Kirby.[1] My debt to him will be apparent to all informed readers, but my approach is rather different – sufficiently so, I hope, to warrant another study. Earlier literature is listed in the bibliography. The unpublished source material for the study starts with the considerable quantity of Pease family papers, some in the possession of Mr J. Gurney Pease to whom (and to whose wife) I am grateful for much assistance and most generous hospitality. More family papers are in the Durham County Record Office, along with other important local collections. The county archivist Mr David Butler and his staff have at all times been helpful, welcoming and efficient, as have the staffs of the Cleveland, Northumberland, North Yorkshire and Tyne and Wear record offices. Mr Tommy Moore of Consett helped me with records of the Consett Iron Company. The House of Lords Record Office staff guided me through parliamentary records. The Public Record Office were helpful with business records. The staff of the various libraries where I have worked, in Durham, Edinburgh, London and Oxford, have as ever been resourceful and helpful. Former colleagues in the Department of History, University of Durham, have been generous with their expertise in economic and local history. Finally but by no means least, I wish to thank two friends. Dr Margaret Harvey suggested to me an entirely new field of research at a point when my previous main area of study had ceased to offer new attractions; and she has lived with the Peases while I worked on them. Cherry Dowrick (a Friend) has illuminated Quakerism for me and enlarged my understanding of Quaker history.

PICTURE ACKNOWLEDGMENTS

Plate 1 is reproduced by permission of the National Portrait Gallery; plates 2, 3, 6, 9, 10 and 18 by permission of Darlington Library and Art Gallery; plates 4 and 5 by permission of the National Railway Museum; plate 7 by permission of J. Gurney Pease; plate 8 by permission of Darlington Borough Art Collection; plate 11, from T. H. Hair, *Views of the Colleries in the Counties of Northumberland and Durham*, by permission of Durham University Library; plates 12 and 13 by permission of Middlesbrough Central Library; plate 14 by permission of Teesside Archives; plate 17, from a negative in the possession of Mr H. Abrams, 1975, by permission of Durham Record Office. Plates 15 and 16 are from photographs by the author.

---

[1]   Especially *Men of Business and Politics. The Rise and Fall of the Quaker Pease Business Dynasty of North-East England, 1700–1943*, London 1984; *The Origins of Railway Enterprise. Stockton and Darlington Railway 1821*, Cambridge 1993.

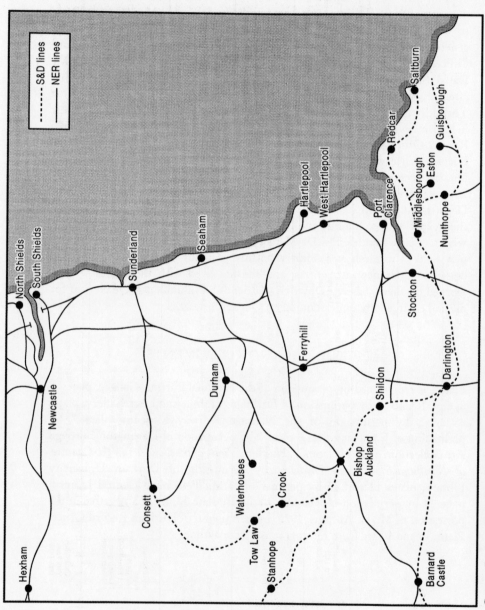

County Durham and Cleveland railway network in 1863

Legend:
- S&D lines
- NER lines

Hexham, Newcastle, North Shields, South Shields, Sunderland, Seaham, Hartlepool, West Hartlepool, Port Clarence, Redcar, Saltburn, Guisborough, Eston, Middlesborough, Nunthorpe, Stockton, Darlington, Shildon, Bishop Auckland, Ferryhill, Durham, Consett, Waterhouses, Crook, Tow Law, Stanhope, Barnard Castle

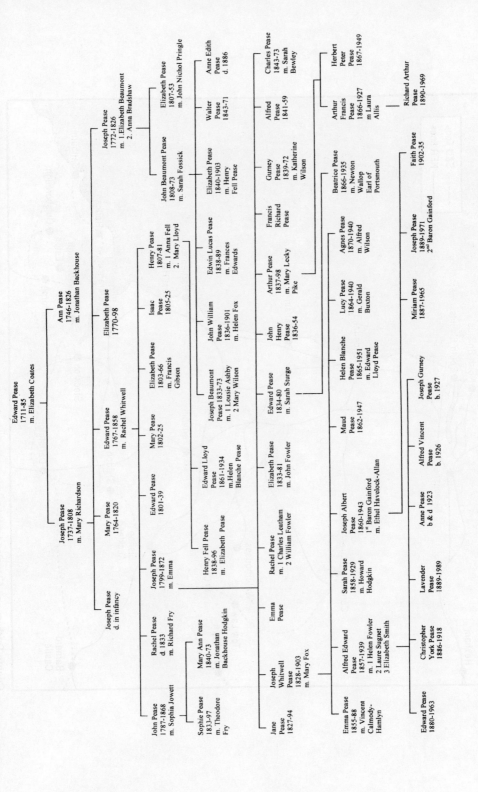

CHAPTER ONE
Family and Religion

The connection of the Pease family with Darlington began in the first half of the eighteenth century. The family appears to have originated in Essex; but by the end of the seventeenth century they were established as small landowners in the West Riding of Yorkshire. Joseph Pease, who was born in 1685, married in 1706 Ann Couldwell, heiress of two brothers who were wool-combers in Darlington.[1] Their eldest son Joseph inherited the property in Yorkshire; the second son Edward, born in 1711, joined his uncles' business in Darlington and took it over in 1760. A family story had it that Edward was turned out of his home for becoming a Quaker; but since he was only eight years old when his father died, and his mother was of Quaker stock, this does not seem likely. But at any rate it seems clear that although Edward was baptised, he was a Quaker by 1735, when he married Elizabeth Coates, a member of a local Quaker family, at Raby meeting house.[2]

When Edward Pease joined it, the Couldwell wool-combing business largely consisted of organising production by workers in their homes. But from 1752 an increasing amount of work, not only sorting and combing the wool but also weaving and dying, was done at a mill in Priestgate, Darlington, and a smaller mill in the Leadyard.[3] Edward died in 1785, leaving the woollen business to his eldest son Joseph and the remainder of his property, including houses in Darlington and amounting in value to some £3000, divided equally between his five sons and two daughters.[4] This Joseph Pease, born in 1737, expanded the woollen enterprise and set up a banking business. This was not an unusual step among industrialists, especially those engaged in textile and metal businesses, at a time when the currency system was unreliable and a local bank could help to provide local means of payment and finance the

---

[1]   Joseph Foster, *Pease of Darlington*, privately published 1891, p. 4; Sir Alfred E. Pease, *The Diaries of Edward Pease, the Father of English Railways*, London 1907, p. 43.

[2]   Durham County Record Office (henceforth DCRO), SF/St/MM 1 /2: Raby Monthly Meeting, 4 Jun, 20 Jul. 1735.

[3]   Henry Pease and Co., *Bi-centenary 1752–1952. Priestgate Mills, Darlington*, Darlington 1952.

[4]   DCRO, D/XD/5/300, Edward Pease's will, 1785; Kirby, *Men of Business and Politics*, p. 2.

waiting between various stages of manufacture, payment to suppliers, and receipt of payment from customers.[5] Pease's bank never issued notes, and remained an adjunct of the family's industrial enterprises, whereas another Darlington bank, set up by the Backhouse family in 1774, became a purely banking concern. Joseph Pease's son Edward, born in 1767, was the one who added other industrial interests to the woollen business.

Edward Pease had evidently built up a sizeable fortune by 1818 when, instead of retiring from business as he had been contemplating, he embarked on the promotion of the Stockton and Darlington Railway, invested substantially in it, and became one of the pioneers of a new transport system. Edward had a reputation as an austere and rigorous businessman;[6] but over the railway he revealed gifts of imagination that went well beyond the type of the 'safe money-maker.' He devoted much of his time over the next ten years to the railway and the locomotive-building firm of Robert Stephenson and Co., for which he provided half the capital, only finally retiring in 1827. Even after that he took an interest in his sons' business, came to the rescue in the crisis of 1847–8, and lived to see the beginning of a new family enterprise and a new era of railway consolidation.

The careers of Edward Pease, his second son Joseph (born 1799) and his eldest grandson Joseph Whitwell (born 1828) span the whole of the nineteenth century. These three men were of prime importance in the history of the family businesses, but many of the male members of the family worked in them, and most were active in the affairs of Darlington. Edward Pease's younger brother Joseph (known, to differentiate him from his father and his nephew, as Joseph Pease of Feethams, his house in the centre of Darlington) took charge of the woollen mills. His son John Beaumont Pease withdrew from business on account of poor health, and thereafter lived to the age of seventy, active in local affairs.

Edward Pease had five sons, two of whom died comparatively young and did not make a mark on the business. The eldest son, John, devoted most of his energies to the Quaker ministry and travelled frequently on it; but he remained a partner, was consulted by his brothers,[7] and took part in negotiations such as those for the merger of the Stockton and Darlington Railway and the North Eastern Railway in 1859–60. He also took a full share in Darlington affairs. The youngest son, Henry, in turn took charge of the woollen mills but was also active in railway development. He was particularly associated with the line from Barnard Castle over Stainmoor to Tebay, and

[5]   L. S. Pressnell, *Country Banking in the Industrial Revolution*, Oxford 1956, pp. 14–21.

[6]   Francis Mewburn, *Memoir of Fra: Mewburn, Chief Bailiff of Darlington and First Railway Solicitor, by his Son*, Darlington 1867, pp. 61–2.

[7]   E.g. Joseph Pease diary, 14 May, 25 Aug., 8 Nov., 20 Nov. 1847, J. G.Pease Papers.

also with the line from Redcar to Saltburn, whose development as a seaside resort he fostered. Eventually Henry became wholly occupied with the Darlington section of the North Eastern Railway. He was also active in Darlington affairs and, farther afield, in the peace movement, going on a mission to Russia in 1854 to try to avert the war impending over the Crimea.[8]

The leading businessman in this generation was Edward Pease's second son Joseph. He was a true entrepreneur. It was Joseph who launched the family colliery business and built it up to an annual production of over one million tons by the time of his death. He took every opportunity to expand the Stockton and Darlington railway network, and was capable of a distant vision of the future for Middlesbrough. He was prepared to venture into Parliament in 1832, the first Quaker to do so. Joseph's readiness to embrace new enterprises sometimes strained his finances, but on the whole his speculations were based on careful calculation, his credit never failed, and his capacity to do the work of two or three ordinary men was said to be due not only to enormous energy but to methodical habits and administrative ability. Joseph Pease's business enemies impugned his motives and character, but there is no record of charges of dishonesty. At the age of twenty-one Joseph drew up the first prospectus for the Stockton and Darlington Railway; he became its treasurer in 1833 and shortly afterwards chairman of the management committee. In the 1850s the family-owned business interests were reorganised into separate companies. Two were concerned with minerals: Joseph Pease and Partners with the collieries and the related activities of coke ovens and the manufacture of fire bricks; and J. W. Pease and Co. set up to exploit Cleveland ironstone and limestone products. The woollen business was now entitled Henry Pease and Co. There was also the Middlesbrough Estate, which by 1858 was entirely owned by members of the Pease family. Finally there was the private banking firm of J. and J. W. Pease, which was in effect the finance department for the various family enterprises and the railway. All this, with important shareholdings in the Stockton and Darlington Railway and its related lines (and from 1860 the North Eastern Railway) amounted to a very substantial industrial empire. Joseph Pease died in 1872 a very rich man, leaving an estate of over £300,000.[9]

The next generation grew up in an atmosphere of expansion and increasing affluence, but most of the men went into one or other branch of the business. The deaths of three of Joseph Pease's sons, however, reduced the number of potential partners and affected the finances. Gurney started in the ironstone business but died in 1872 aged thirty-two, leaving a young family. Charles died in 1873 at the age of thirty: his only son died as a child a few

8   Mary H. Pease, *Henry Pease. A Short Story of His Life*, London 1897, pp. 47–66; Joseph Sturge, *Some Account of a Deputation from the ... Society of Friends to the Emperor of Russia*, London 1854.

9   Kirby, *Men of Business*, p. 45.

years later. Edward went into the woollen mill but his health was not robust, and by the time of his marriage he had all but given up business. Instead he travelled a good deal and bought an estate in Worcestershire where he experimented with forestry and the breeding of mules.[10] Edward died in 1880, leaving a fourteen-year-old daughter whose financial affairs were to cost the family dear.

After the deaths of Charles and Gurney Pease the surviving brothers contemplated selling the mining enterprises, but instead decided to take in new blood and offered a partnership in these firms to David Dale. Dale was an early Pease protégé, a Quaker, now a successful businessman in his own right, managing director of the Consett Iron Company and of the Darlington section of the North Eastern Railway. He had a national reputation as a pioneer of arbitration in industrial relations.[11] It was largely due to Dale's influence that in 1882 the colliery, ironstone and limestone branches of the Pease businesses were combined in a new private company under the name of Pease and Partners, with a capital of £2.25 million, Joseph Whitwell Pease as chairman and Dale as managing director.[12] The principal partners were now Joseph Pease's surviving sons Joseph Whitwell and Arthur. In addition Henry Pease's son Henry Fell, whilst chiefly concerned with the woollen mills, was a partner in the reorganised colliery and ironstone company, as was John Beaumont Pease's third son Edwin Lucas. John Beaumont Pease's second son John William (known as John William Pease of Pendower) moved to Newcastle and became a partner in a different bank. Family relations remained close, because he married a sister of Joseph Whitwell Pease's wife, but his descendants were not concerned with the Pease businesses.

Joseph Whitwell Pease, as his father's eldest son and the major shareholder in the businesses, was to bear the main responsibility for the family fortunes for thirty years. He entered the banking branch at the age of seventeen, and in the reorganisation of the 1850s became a partner in the colliery company and the bank, while the ironstone and limestone company of J. W. Pease was created as his particular sphere. Joseph Whitwell was also active in railway affairs, taking part in the expansion of the Stockton and Darlington Railway network and in the merger negotiations with the North Eastern Railway. He became one of the three members of the Stockton and Darlington management committee to be made a director of the North

[10]   A. E. Pease, 'Autobiographical Record,' pp. 29–30, J. G.Pease Papers.

[11]   Kirby, *Men of Business*, pp. 77–8; Sir David Dale, *Thirty Years Experience of Industrial Conciliation and Arbitration*, London 1899; Sir Edward Grey, *Sir David Dale. Inaugural Address delivered for the Dale Memorial Trust, to which is prefaced a Memoir by Howard Pease*, London 1911.

[12]   Kirby, *Men of Business*, p. 78; Joseph Gurney Pease, ed., *A Wealth of Happiness and Many Bitter Trials. The Journals of Sir Alfred Pease, a Restless Man*, York 1992, pp. 18–19.

Eastern Railway, and eventually became its chairman in 1894. He sat in Parliament from 1865 until his death in 1903, and was given a baronetcy in 1882, the first Quaker to receive such an honour as his father had been the first to enter Parliament. By the time he was thirty Joseph Whitwell was trying to take some of the load off his father's shoulders, and he was credited with having brought zeal, courage and financial ability to his father's assistance.[13] But he does not seem to have had his father's or his grandfather's business vision, and he was not good at sharing responsibility. As his brothers died he simply took on more himself, and he did not manage to train his sons to succeed him. The other surviving brother, Arthur, was a full partner, with a smaller shareholding, and also sat in Parliament; but he was a less dominant figure in the business.

Joseph Whitwell's two sons, Alfred Edward and Joseph Albert (generally known as Jack) both went into the business as did Arthur's sons. Alfred went reluctantly into the banking branch, Jack into the colliery side. Both were made partners, but neither was given a full insight into their potential obligations. Alfred disliked the industry that had made his family's name and financed the country pursuits and the travels that he loved, writing later: 'I disliked from childhood the spoiling industrial hand of my family, who thought they were doing good work in providing more and more employment for the people. I could see as a boy that the more they did this, the more families of boys would be produced for whom more and more mines and pits and factories would have to be made, till our lovely world would be ash heaps and chimneys and hideous houses under smoke clouds.'[14] As a director of Pease and Partners Alfred found his advice ignored,[15] and it may be that frustration at his father's reluctance to give him responsibility influenced his decision to give up active work in the banking branch in the 1890s in order to travel for the sake of his wife's health – she suffered from a lung infection and they spent much of every winter abroad until 1902. Alfred loved the travel, especially in remote parts (Switzerland bored him), and he was conscious in himself of 'a want of systematic work – my constant tendency to idleness.'[16] He was not a seriously ambitious man, either in business or in politics. After being returned to Parliament in 1897, in

[13] J. W. Pease to John Pease, 1 Feb. 1858, DCRO, Hodgkin Papers, D/Ho/C 52/269; *Friends Quarterly Examiner* 38 (1904), pp. 175–84.

[14] A. E. Pease, 'Autobiographical Record,' J. G. Pease Papers; Pease, *Wealth of Happiness*, p. 5.

[15] A. E. Pease, 'Autobiographical Record', pp. 228–36, J. G. Pease Papers; Pease, *Wealth of Happiness*, pp. 15–16, 19, 61; Kirby, *Men of Business*, p. 85.

[16] A. E. Pease journal, 31 Dec. 1886, J. G. Pease Papers; Pease, *Wealth of Happiness*, p. 52. Alfred wrote a number of books on his travels and on wild life and became something of an authority on Africa. He also edited Edward Pease's diaries and wrote a book of political reminiscences.

his absence and against his inclination, he did not feel obliged to attend the House of Commons in the early months of each year.

Sir Joseph Pease may have regarded his second son as his eventual business heir, giving him, for example, a salary as a director of Pease and Partners while Alfred received none. Alfred resented this favouritism, and did not think Jack worked much harder in the business than he did himself.[17] Jack also pursued a more ambitious political career, giving it higher priority than business and reaching heights not scaled by his father. He did, however, return to Pease and Partners after the crisis of 1902.

The Stockton and Darlington Railway was known as the Quaker line: some 75% of the original capital came from within the Society of Friends. Darlington became known as the Quaker town, owing to the predominance of the Peases and other Quaker families. The local football club is still known as the Quakers. Quakerism was important to the Pease family and gave a particular colour to their position and reputation. To appreciate this it is necessary to consider the position of Quakerism in nineteenth-century English society.

Quakers were prominent in the financial development and industrial-isation of England in the eighteenth and early nineteenth century, out of all proportion to their numbers in the population. Some writers have discussed the reasons for this prominence in religious terms, but it is difficult to find reasons in Quakers' beliefs that disposed them more towards economic enterprise or brought them success more than members of other sects which also stressed individual responsibility and endeavour.[18] There do, however, seem to be some social factors that apply particularly to the Society of Friends over and above those common to all Dissenters.

The first period of Quakerism, from George Fox's missionary ventures in 1647, was marked by enthusiasm, confrontation, and persecution. Quakers stressed personal spiritual experience. All mankind had the light of Christ if they would recognise it; all were fallen sinners, but all could be saved if they ceased to resist the inner workings of the light. Priests and sacraments were not necessary; even the Bible, although very important, was not the fountain of all truth and knowledge. Pure religion, in the words of the Epistle of James (1:27) was 'to visit the fatherless and widows in their affliction, and to keep himself unspotted from the world.' Works, especially concern for the poor, were therefore central; and to remain in tune with the light required constant watchfulness and diligence. Keeping oneself unspotted from the world meant rejection of secular hierarchy and marks of social deference, refusal to swear oaths (another scriptural injunction: James 5:12), and plain dress, speech and

---

[17] A. E. Pease journal, 14 Jun. 1901, J. G. Pease Papers.

[18] See for example David H. Pratt, *English Quakers and the First Industrial Revolution*, New York and London 1985, ch. 1; Michael R. Watts, *The Dissenters*, Vol. 2, Oxford 1995, pp. 327–55.

lifestyle. War was a consequence and cause of sin; whilst early Quakers were often belligerent in speech, refusal to take up arms soon became standard. These attitudes brought much persecution under the Commonwealth and especially under the restored monarchy: Fox himself was imprisoned nine times.[19] Persecution subsided at the end of the seventeenth century, and with it the expectation of an early vindication and desire for confrontation with the world. The Quakers became quietist, concentrating on the self-contained community and individual spiritual development.

Unlike some of the puritan sects of the mid-seventeenth century, Quaker individualism was never anarchic: it was accompanied and controlled by a strong instinct for community and consensus. All could participate equally in the silent meeting for worship, but in the monthly and quarterly district meetings decisions had to be reached by consensus. The yearly meeting in London was open to all Friends. Each local meeting had a scheme of poor relief. As members of a small community, better-off Quakers were expected to, and did, provide apprenticeships and credit for young Friends wanting to go into business. Friends' conduct in business was carefully watched over: the unfortunate might be helped; but irresponsible behaviour or negligence could lead to expulsion (disownment).[20] The structure of regional and yearly meetings, along with travel, provided opportunities to meet potential business, and marriage, partners. Marriage outside the Society led to disownment; marriage within it strengthened social and business solidarity.

The Quakers were never a large body, but at the beginning of the eighteenth century their numbers, estimated at 39,510, about 0.73% of the population of England, compared well with those of other Dissenting groups. There were 696 Meetings, more than the number of Presbyterian chapels and more than those of Independents and Baptists put together. During the eighteenth and early nineteenth century numbers declined. In 1773 there were 563 Meetings; an unofficial census in 1840 recorded a membership of 16,227; the 1851 religious census recorded 16,783 attendances at 363 meetings.[21]

[19] For the history of Quakerism to about 1700 see W. C. Braithwaite, *The Second Period of Quakerism*, 2nd edn Cambridge 1961; R. Vann, *The Social Development of English Quakerism*, Cambridge MA 1969; Michael R. Watts, *The Dissenters*, Vol. 1, Oxford 1978, chs. 2 and 3. A recent survey of the whole history, with particular reference to business activity, is James Walvin, *The Quakers. Money and Morals*, London 1997.

[20] Stephen Allott, *Friends in York, The Quaker Story in the Life of a Meeting*, York 1978, pp. 56-9; Ann Prior and Maurice Kirby, 'The Society of Friends and business culture, 1700-1830,' in David J. Jeremy, ed., *Religion, Business and Wealth in Modern Britain*, London and New York 1998, pp. 115-36, give examples of detailed supervision exercised by meetings in the eighteenth century. For an example in Newcastle in the mid-nineteenth century see below, p. 39.

[21] Watts, *Dissenters*, Vol. 1, pp. 270, 386-90; Vol. 2, pp. 23-4, 27-9.

During the eighteenth and well into the nineteenth century all Dissenters were subject to legal disabilities. The worst of the penal laws of the Restoration were suspended by the Toleration Act of 1689, but the Test and Corporation Acts remained in force, making the holding of public and municipal office dependent on receiving the sacrament according to the rites of the Church of England. Some Dissenters felt able to conform occasionally and thus qualify for local office – there was, for example, a succession of Presbyterians in the mayoralty of Nottingham; but other sects discouraged the practice. National politics were virtually closed: in the century after 1714 there were never more than five Dissenters in Parliament at any one time.[22] Dissenters could not go to English universities. Whilst the Schism Act that limited their opening of schools was repealed in 1718, chapels and ministers had to be licensed by magistrates. Dissenters were obliged to pay tithes to the owners and incumbents of Church of England livings. Various acts of Parliament from the 1690s simplified the procedure for the recovery of tithes by distress, but the justices were not obliged to follow the procedure, and clergy could and did take people to the ecclesiastical courts. Church rates were levied on all the occupiers of property in a parish. They were spent on maintaining the fabric of the parish church, paying the clerk's salary, and providing vestments, bells, prayer books and other materials for the services, and might pay for heating and lighting.[23]

Church rates and tithes were a permanent grievance, the more so when goods greatly exceeding in value the sums due were seized under a distraint warrant. Enforcement became harsher from the 1790s with increasing Anglican and judicial hostility to Dissenters, an increase due to fear of political radicalism and revolution. Objections to church rates became more vocal after 1818, when political paranoia began to subside, when pressure for repeal of the Test and Corporation Acts was growing, and when at the same time the government gave £1.5 million for a programme of Anglican church building to meet growth of population and changes in its distribution. Attempts were made to force ratepayers to pay for the upkeep of the new as well as the old churches. There were three possible ways of resisting compulsory church rates. One was to obtain their abolition by act of Parliament: this was tried from 1834 onwards, but a series of government and private bills was defeated in the House of Lords. The second course was to take control of the parish vestry and stop rates being levied: this was possible because all ratepayers, whether churchgoers or not, had the right to attend the vestry meeting. This course was increasingly followed from the 1830s, and in

---

22   Watts, *Dissenters*, Vol. 1, pp. 482–3; Vol. 2, p. 348.
23   Watts, *Dissenters*, Vol. 1, pp. 476–85, 587–9; G. I. T. Machin, *Politics and the Churches in Great Britain 1832 to 1868*, Oxford 1977, pp. 18–19; J. P. Ellens, *Religious Routes to Gladstonian Liberalism. The Church Rate Conflict in England and Wales, 1832–1868*, University Park, PA 1994, ch. 1.

large towns rates were often abandoned. In Manchester, for example, rates having been rejected by the ratepayers in 1835 were never levied again; but struggles continued elsewhere until 1868, with some notorious cases in the 1840s and 50s. The third possible course, to which these struggles contributed, was to publicise the injustice of compelling Dissenters to support the established church and seizing their goods. By doing so, it was hoped, the establishment would be shamed into dropping the rates. This campaign was, however, complicated rather than helped by becoming involved with one to disestablish the Church of England altogether.[24]

All these disabilities applied to all Dissenters. The position of the Quakers was special in some further respects. Their refusal to swear oaths meant initially that they could not give evidence in courts of law. A series of acts of parliament from 1696, made permanent in 1721, allowed Quakers to affirm instead of taking the oath in civil cases; but they were still precluded from giving evidence in criminal cases, from sitting on juries, and from holding any office or position of profit under the Crown. Their rejection of sacraments meant that they could not practise occasional conformity for the sake of holding municipal office. Their pacifism prevented them from joining the army or navy. They were, however, along with Jews, exempted by Hardwicke's Marriage Act of 1753 from the requirement that all marriages had to be solemnised in church according to the rites of the Church of England. As quiet people the Quakers did not on the whole join with other Dissenters in pressure-group politics. They did not belong to the Dissenting Deputies, representatives of old Dissent in the London area who were unofficial leaders in relations with government and Parliament. When in 1836 tithes were commuted into a rent charge some Quakers did not refuse to pay, against the wishes of the Yearly Meeting. With church rates they would not cooperate, and recorded the sums exacted annually in the Book of Sufferings; but they did not actively resist demands made in lawful form. In 1796, for example, John Richardson, a tanner in North Shields, wrote to a local magistrate that he submitted to the law out of duty, but the fact that he had recently had leather worth over £2 and £3 3s. 9d. siezed for charges of 15s. and £1 5s. 8d. respectively would go down in the record of sufferings.[25] In 1839, after the failure of the first attempt to get church rates abolished by Parliament, the Dissenters of Darlington issued a joint address which, although not signed, is evidently of Quaker origin. The expenditure of a rate, it said, was not for the community at large. It neither was sanctioned by Christianity nor had any reference to the 'things which are Caesar's' which Christians should properly pay. 'Why ask the Baptist, the Independent, or the

[24] Ellens, *Religious Routes to Gladstonian Liberalism*, passim; Machin, *Politics and the Churches*, pp. 103–07, 259–60, 349–55; Watts, *Dissenters*, Vol. 2, pp. 587–9.
[25] George Richardson, *Annals of the Cleveland Richardsons and their Descendants. Compiled from Family Manuscripts*, Newcastle upon Tyne 1850, pp. 86–8.

Friend, to contribute to a font, a communion table, or a surplice? ... Other Christian societies are cheerfully laying out their thousands to build chapels, to maintain ministers, missionaries, or their own poor, whilst you [members of the established church] with such few incumbrances are continually goading us for trifles, beneath our notice in amount, and yet of consequence on account of the great injustice which makes the claim, and the principle involved in the payment.' Distraint made legally should be suffered peaceably. 'We do not war with Episcopacy; let those who believe it the most scriptural form of church government continue to enjoy it in peace, but let not a whole nation rich and poor be taxed for its trappings. We sincerely respect and wish well to all Christians from the "ceremonious Romanist" to the "plain Friend" provided their conduct promotes peace on earth and good will to men.' The address had no immediate effect. As late as 1851, when Quakers were said to dominate Darlington, thirty-nine of their number had goods seized for church rates; but that does seem to have been the last year the rates were levied.[26]

The social standing of English Quakers in the first half of the nineteenth century was on the whole higher than that of other Dissenters. Commentators of all kinds, from Friedrich Engels onwards, have long asserted the essentially bourgeois character of Victorian Nonconformity, and its failure, like that of the established church, to attract substantial support from the poorer classes. This generalisation, it now seems, will not altogether stand up to statistical analysis. In the late seventeenth and early eighteenth century Dissent did appeal chiefly to the economically independent, neither the aristocracy nor the labouring classes but those in between.[27] But with the evangelical revival and the great expansion of Dissent the picture changes, so that by the 1820s and 30s in the great majority of English counties the membership of the evangelical Dissenting bodies was predominantly poor, agricultural labourers, depressed urban workers, and miners. If the 1851 census revealed that nearly half the population did not attend any place of worship on the Sunday in question, and suggested that the majority of the absentees were labourers and artisans, the evidence of the Dissenting registers is that the majority of those who did attend were working class too.[28]

To this pattern the Quakers and the Unitarians did not fully conform. Early Quakers, like other Dissenters, seem to have been predominantly economically independent, and included a number of small gentry, many substantial farmers, and wholesale traders, but few unskilled labourers. There was no spectacular change after 1700, although the number of gentry

---

[26] Address to 'the conscientious Members of the Establishment and to all Dissenters of all classes in the Town of Darlington,' 1839, DCRO, D/XD/10/9; handbill, 28 Sep. 1840, D/XD/10/10; Darlington Monthly Meeting, Record of Sufferings, SF/Da/MM 7/3.

[27] Watts, *Dissenters*, Vol. 1, pp. 346–54.

[28] Watts, *Dissenters*, Vol. 2, pp. 303–27.

declined.[29] In general in the late eighteenth and early nineteenth century conversion, and membership of a Dissenting sect, evidently produced a conscientious attitude to work and a rejection of frivolous pursuits: hard work and saving could then bring modest prosperity. But modest prosperity and respectability are one thing, outstanding business enterprise and wealth are another; and in the middle of the nineteenth century Quakers and Unitarians were heavily over-represented among the very rich. There were nearly ten times as many Unitarians among millionaires and half millionaires as there were in the population as a whole, and fifty times as many Quakers.[30] The list of major firms founded by Quakers includes the Backhouses, Barclays, Gurneys and Lloyds in banking, Darby in iron-making, the Peases in railways and coal, the Ransomes in agricultural machinery, the Clarks in shoe-making, Huntley and Palmer and Carrs in biscuits, Rowntrees, Cadburys and Frys in chocolate and cocoa.

Exclusion from public and political life and from the universities made business the obvious occupation for all Dissenters. Added to this, the geographical distribution and social structure of Dissent over the century before the industrial revolution often put Quakers and Unitarians in a good position to embrace new opportunities. None of the new major entrepreneurs started from the bottom: each had one or two generations of prosperity and capital behind him. Declining numbers almost seems to have helped, isolation enhancing the instinct for self-preservation and mutual support. In the Quaker case the rule about marrying only within the Society helped to keep money in the family; national and international journeying fostered business as well as religious links. Quaker reputation for probity, and the fact that bankruptcy was always investigated and often visited with disownment does much to explain the trust that non-Quakers as well as Friends placed in Quaker bankers. Two further factors, it is suggested, help to account for Quaker and Unitarian success in business. Unlike the new Methodists and the old Baptist and Independent churches, they were not obsessed with the evangelical endeavour which made the saving of souls the chief priority and absorbed a great deal of energy. And the absence of an ordained and salaried (however humbly) ministry meant that the ablest young men were not drawn away from a business calling at a time when the other Dissenters were setting increasing store by a learned ministry.[31]

The Protestant ethic notwithstanding, puritan teaching was by no means unequivocally favourable to the making of money. Calvin himself denounced usury. Wesley forbade his itinerant preachers to engage in trade, and regarded

[29] Vann, *Social Development of English Quakerism*, pp. 47–87.
[30] Watts, *Dissenters*, Vol. 2, pp. 331–2.
[31] Watts, *Dissenters*, Vol. 2, pp. 327–46. For a study of some prominent Quaker businesses see David Burns Windsor, *The Quaker Enterprise. Friends in Business*, London 1980.

increasing wealth as a potential spiritual danger. In 1763, for example, he warned the brethren in Bristol 'not to "love the world, neither the things of the world." This will be the great danger. As they are industrious and frugal, they must increase in goods.' In his last years Wesley became ever more insistent that it was dangerous to keep more in one's hands than was necessary for one's own household, for carrying on one's business, or for leaving enough to one's children for their necessities. In a sermon of 1780 he warned that Christ forbade laying up treasures on earth as expressly as he forbade adultery or murder; by 1788 he described wealth as a mortal danger to the soul and an obstacle to entry into the kingdom of heaven.[32] The Wesleyan preacher and scholar Adam Clarke replied, to a businessman who complained that on his rigorous principles few commercial men would be saved: 'I cannot help that sir. I may not bring down the requirements of infinite justice to suit the selfish chicanery of any sort of men whatever.' The silk merchant Thomas Wilson wrote in one of his ledgers a text from the Book of Proverbs: 'He that maketh haste to be rich shall not be innocent ... He that hasteth to be rich hath an evil eye.' After hearing in 1794 a series of sermons warning against giving priority to making money, Wilson gave up business and devoted the rest of his life to repairing and building Congregational chapels, and to other good causes such as the London Missionary Society and founding London University.[33]

Quakers and Unitarians were less worried about wealth in itself, regarding it indeed as a blessing from God; but they were equally concerned lest its pursuit lead to idolatry. A tract of 1759 said that to be rich was 'a Situation highly to be prized, as affording Opportunities for religious Retreat and meditation'; the rich could not be condemned if their wealth were 'devoted to the Good of the Community, both civil and religious, and to the Promotion of an honest Industry, and the improvement of useful Arts among the Poor, as well as succouring them in their Distress.' The Yearly Meeting issued regular warnings about moderation in the acquisition and spending of money, as well as about strict integrity in business. In 1741 it said that 'The principal, if not only, satisfaction a man of truly Christian disposition can have, in affluence and the increase of the things of this world, must arise from the greater advantages and opportunities put into his hands of doing good therewith.' The epistle of 1781 repeated a warning that the 'direct tendency' of 'lucrative acquisition' was to 'draw away the mind, and alienate it from the love and fear of God.' Jonathan Backhouse wrote in 1800 that 'the root of the evil is, not so much the *possession* of property ... as in the undue and inordinate *pursuit* of it.' The Yearly Meeting of 1815 feared that 'many who

---

[32]   *The Works of John Wesley*, Nashville 1982 ff., *Sermons*, ed. A. C. Outler, Vol. 2, pp. 263–80, Vol. 3, pp. 228–46, 518–28, Vol. 4, pp. 177–86; *Journals and Diaries*, ed. W. R. Ward and Richard P. Heitzenrater, Vol. 4, p. 428.

[33]   Watts, *Dissenters*, Vol. 2, pp. 333, 339–40; Proverbs 28: 20, 22.

begin the world with moderate views, meeting at first with success in trade, go on extending their commercial concerns, until they become involved therein to a degree prohibited by the precepts of Christ, and incompatible with their own safety.' The banker Joseph John Gurney wrote to his brother in 1839: 'One cannot but feel alarmed at the flow of money ... to which thy letter alludes. But it really does not seem in any way to be of our own seeking and it appears to me that the grand object to aim at under the circumstances, is Divine grace to enable us to be good, faithful and *liberal* stewards, of that which is committed to our charge.'[34]

Philanthropy, and puritanical attitudes to consumption, were moral imperatives for the Victorian middle classes across the denominational spectrum: Quakers were not unique in embracing them. Over the course of the nineteenth century, whilst the principles of Quakerism did not change, many of the outward signs that had earlier marked Friends off from the surrounding society were abandoned, so that by the end of the century they were hardly distinguishable as a separate people.[35] The outpouring, after about 1780, of undenominational evangelical Christianity did little for Quaker numbers (unlike, for example, the Methodists) but profoundly affected individuals and attitudes. A strong strand of quietism continued, but evangelicalism became predominant among Quakers, as among other Dissenters and many Anglicans, until about the 1870s when it began to give way to a more liberal theology. Evangelicalism brought Quakers into closer cooperation with other Christians in undenominational causes such as anti-slavery and temperance. It gave rise to some new practices such as mission meetings with hymn-singing. Some Quakers began to attend evangelical services of other churches in addition to meeting for worship. Younger Friends began to question the concept of peculiarity and the usefulness of some of the rules that separated them from the rest of society. In 1856 Yorkshire Quarterly Meeting, at the instigation of John Stephenson Rowntree, a York grocer, father of the founder of the cocoa firm, introduced a proposal that Quakers should be allowed to retain membership after marrying non-members. After heated debate the proposal was finally adopted by the Yearly Meeting of 1859, as was another proposal, brought up by Joseph Sturge, Birmingham corn merchant, radical and peace campaigner, to make peculiarity of speech and dress optional. The supporters of change were chiefly inspired by anxiety at the decline in numbers in the Society: the marriage rule cost it many otherwise devout and excellent members, and

---

[34] Society of Friends, *Epistles from the Yearly Meeting of Friends, held in London, to the Quarterly and Monthly Meetings in Great Britain, Ireland and Elsewhere; from 1681 to 1857 inclusive*, London 1858, Vol. 1, p. 236; Vol. 2, pp. 46–7, 169; Pratt, *English Quakers and the First Industrial Revolution*, pp. 31–3; David E. Swift, *Joseph John Gurney. Banker, Reformer and Quaker*, Middletown, CT 1962, pp. 86–8.

[35] For all this see Elizabeth Isichei, *Victorian Quakers*, Oxford 1970.

prevented others from marrying at all.[36] Conservatives no longer seriously claimed that marriage in a church or chapel with a non-Quaker meant recognition of a priesthood, or that Quaker dress was now anything other than a uniform. They defended their cause mainly in terms of tradition and utility, were less troubled about declining numbers, and came to fear that by giving up the distinctive forms the Society was losing its sense of identity. The effects of the changes were not abrupt: the traditional usage of 'first day', 'fifth month', etc., was declining before 1860 but was not abandoned overnight; the older generation went on using plain speech and wearing plain dress.[37] But by the 1880s nearly half of all marriages of Quakers were with non-members of the Society.[38]

Apart from distinctive dress and language, Quakers had been from the start bound by various restrictions on consumption and recreation. The injunction to plainness was supposed to apply to their houses; music, even in the home, was condemned as a distraction; gambling and theatre-going were censured; 'vain sports,' hunting and shooting, 'killing the creatures of God for self-gratification,' were deprecated.[39] Actual practice varied widely, and standards of behaviour were gradually modified; but whilst some fifty rules were removed from the Book of Discipline in 1860, a new form of puritanism, teetotalism, came near to being adopted as official teaching. Quakers were involved in the temperance movement from its early stages.[40] The Yearly Meetings of 1830 and 1835 adopted recommendations against the consumption and manufacture of spirits, and involvement in dram shops; but at this stage a distinction was drawn between spirits and beer, and there were a number of Quaker brewers. It was possible to support work to counter the social evils of drinking without feeling obliged to alter one's personal habits of moderation and hospitality. Total abstention spread rapidly in the 1850s and '60s; Yearly Meetings regularly encouraged support for temperance work; in 1874 the Yearly Meeting advised those engaged in the manufacture of any intoxicating drink to consider changing their occupation; and in 1896 Quakers were exhorted to think of becoming teetotalers. By this time, however, interest in the temperance movement in the sense of attempting to

---

[36] John Stephenson Rowntree, *Quakerism Past and Present: being an Inquiry into the Causes of its Decline in Great Britain and Ireland*, London 1859, pp. 153–7.

[37] In dress, avoidance of bright colours and all ornamentation, plain bonnet for women; in speech, use of 'thee' rather than 'you' for the second person singular pronoun, avoidance of honorific forms of address and of heathen names for days of the week and months.

[38] *The Friend*, 25(1885), p. 145.

[39] Society of Friends, *Epistles from the Yearly Meeting*, passim. The advice against field sports was repeated as late as 1883: Society of Friends, *Yearly Meeting Proceedings*, 1883.

[40] For the whole subject see Brian Harrison, *Drink and the Victorians. The Temperance Question in England 1815–1872*, London 1971.

influence public policy was declining. A new generation of Quakers was becoming increasingly concerned with structural causes of poverty and other social problems, for which drink was no longer regarded as a sufficient explanation, nor personal philanthropy a sufficient treatment.

A cause with which, given their principles, Quakers were always closely associated was peace. Friends were never a majority in Victorian pacifist groups; but some, including Joseph Pease of Feethams, were instrumental in founding the Peace Society in 1816 and it was three Friends, Joseph Sturge, William Allen, and Henry Pease, who visited Russia in 1854 to try to prevent the Crimean War. Later in the century the Peace Society was increasingly dominated by Quakers, and its presidency became almost a Pease family tradition. Quakers were active alongside others in advocating arbitration as a means of resolving international disputes. At the level of personal conduct, after the end of the Napoleonic wars refusal to bear arms was not a serious cause of difficulty. Quakers were in theory liable to be called up for the militia, but the ballot was seldom exercised: the militia was in effect a volunteer force. Quakers opposed bills to put the militia on a more solid foundation, and deplored the volunteer rifle societies that grew up from the 1850s; but the number who had goods distrained for refusing to pay a rate for the militia was small compared with the numbers affected by church rates. Whilst the principle of refusing to take up arms was never publicly questioned, the extent to which Quakers should refuse to deal with the armed forces was not laid down, and it did not need to be clarified for forty years after the Crimea. In the Napoleonic wars some Quaker shipowners chartered vessels to the government for military purposes while others armed their ships, and were disowned for doing so. In 1853 Edward Pease refused to accept his share of the profits Robert Stephenson and Co. made from building engines for warships for the King of Sardinia; but in the Crimean War the Clarks of Street felt able to supply sheepskin coats for the soldiers. There was no further serious test until the Boer War. Then George Cadbury refused to tender to supply cocoa for the army in South Africa, but deferred to Queen Victoria's request that he should supply chocolate for her Christmas present to the troops – on terms that precluded personal profit.[41] The Boer War exposed divisions among Friends about adherence to the principle of pacifism when Britain's security was in question, and it proved very difficult to reach an official view. An even harder test came in 1914. Many Quakers joined up, and many resigned even if they were not disowned. Others were reinforced in their pacifism, and found new sacrificial ways of serving humanity.

[41] Anne Ogden Boyce, *Records of a Quaker Family. The Richardsons of Cleveland*, London 1889, pp. 118–19; *The Friend*, 16 (1858), p. 121; *Diaries of Edward Pease*, p. 303; George Barry Sutton, *C. & J. Clark 1833–1903. A History of Shoemaking in Street, Somerset*, York 1979, p. 8; A. G. Gardiner, *Life of George Cadbury*, London 1923, p. 309.

Standards of consumption among the Victorian middle classes, whatever their religious affiliation, changed and were modified over time; and the numbers and wealth of the business class grew, especially in the second half of the century.[42] Generalisation about lifestyle over the class as a whole is dangerous; and for the most part it is difficult to distinguish Quaker businessmen as a group from others of their class. The most important source of new wealth, throughout the century, was finance and trade, rather than manufacturing, and it was predominantly located in London. Tyneside and Teesside produced, between 1858 and 1899, fourteen men who left over £500,000 in personal property as against 131 from the City of London. Only a handful of colliery owners reached that level: Joseph Pease was not among them, but was on the next rung.[43]

Few newly wealthy businessmen used their wealth at once to buy land and status. In the eighteenth century land had been the most secure investment for new money, and offered a sure way to social and political advantage. Landed wealth remained closely connected with social status and political power until about 1880, but only a minority of businessmen bought land on a large scale or put a substantial part of their wealth into land. There were a number of reasons for this. There were now plenty of non-landed investment opportunities, more rewarding after the agricultural depression; men with growing businesses mostly reinvested their profits in their own companies; they tended to divide their property among their children rather than favouring primogeniture; many of them were Liberal in politics and had grown up in an atmosphere hostile to the landed interest. On the whole, in the first generation at least, they did not aspire to join the landed classes.

Nor, in the first generation, did they aspire to high social and political status. The House of Lords remained a centre of political power until just before the First World War: as late as 1905 between one third and half of Cabinet ministers were peers. Until about 1880 ownership of land was virtually a precondition for the grant of a peerage: an unlanded national hero such as Nelson or Wellington could be ennobled, but was also given large grants of public money to buy land with which to support the title. Only two of the non-landed half-millionaires who died between 1809 and 1879 had been

---

[42] For detailed discussion see the work of W. D. Rubinstein: *Men of Property. The Very Wealthy in Britain since the Industrial Revolution*, London 1981; *Elites and the Wealthy in Modern British History*, Brighton 1987; 'Businessmen into Landowners: the question revisited,' in *Land and Society in Britain, 1700–1914. Essays in Honour of F. M. L. Thompson*, ed. Negley Harte and Roland Quincault, Manchester 1996.

[43] Rubinstein, *Men of Property*, pp. 76–8; Rubinstein in *Land and Society*, p. 103; Kirby, *Men of Business*, p. 45. It has to be remembered that Rubinstein's figures are derived from wills, property left at death, and so do not cover men who gave away large sums during their lifetime. Joseph Pease's lifetime benefactions, however, would not put him in a higher category.

given peerages. From the 1880s the number rose: thirty-eight members of business families were given titles in the 1880s and 90s. Baronetcies, rare among such men before 1879, also became more numerous. But whilst ownership of land became less essential for a peerage, some form of political and especially parliamentary service was still a very important prerequisite. Before the 1870s comparatively few businessmen went into Parliament: before the advent of limited liability in the Companies Act of 1862 very few could afford the time to do so. The class basis of political power shifted only very slowly before 1914.

Wealthy businessmen for the most part enjoyed their rising standard of living in their own way, not joining the gentry or aristocracy but sharing some of their pastimes. They built large comfortable suburban houses with handsome gardens; some developed intellectual and artistic interests; they travelled; a good many took up country sports. New forms of business organisation that separated capital ownership from management freed those who did not relish business life from the necessity of constant involvement. Quaker business families do not seem to have differed in these respects from others of their class. There was a wide range of behaviour, and even within one family different members moved at different speeds. It seems, however, from a recent analysis, that only a minority of partners in major Quaker firms remained 'plain' down to 1914 and later.[44] That minority included two of the most notable families, the Rowntrees and the Cadburys. Both Joseph Rowntree and George Cadbury built up highly successful businesses, pioneered new methods of production and management, devoted great attention to the welfare of their employees, maintained a relatively austere lifestyle, gave personal time and energy to Quaker causes, and succeeded in passing on to their sons both business acumen and principles of hard work, lack of worldly ambition, and social responsibility. Both believed that great wealth was more often a curse to a family than a blessing, and both left a large proportion of their personal fortunes to trusts for social purposes.[45] But the Rowntrees and the Cadburys were exceptional. Their record is neither exclusively nor typically Quaker. Many Nonconformist businessmen made large benefactions to their communities and to religious and social causes. To take only one example, the Unitarian Liverpool merchant William Rathbone was another who distrusted great wealth. He started by giving one tenth of his income to the welfare of others, and increased the proportion as his income

[44]   T. A. B. Corley, 'How Quakers coped with business success: Quaker industrialists 1860–1914,' in David J. Jeremy, ed., *Business and Religion in Britain*, Aldershot 1988, pp. 164–205.

[45]   Anne Vernon, *A Quaker Businessman. The Life of Joseph Rowntree 1836–1935*, York 1982; Robert Fitzgerald, *Rowntree and the Marketing Revolution 1862–1969*, Cambridge 1995; Gardiner, *Life of George Cadbury*; Iolo A. Williams, *The Firm of Cadbury 1831–1931*, London 1931.

grew. He wrote to his wife in 1869: 'My feeling with a merchant was that when he got over £200,000 he was too rich for the Kingdom of Heaven.'[46] And on the other hand it became more common among the second or third generation of wealthy businessmen, Quakers and others, to give up active interest in business, to buy country properties for recreation, and gradually to adopt the habits of the gentry. Some of the Quakers concerned remained Friends, albeit of a more worldly kind than their parents and grandparents; some resigned; many of their children married out.[47] Members of the Pease family, as will be seen in a later chapter, fit well in their various ways into this general picture.

[46]   Sheila Marriner, *Rathbones of Liverpool*, Liverpool 1961, p. 4; Watts, *Dissenters*, Vol. 2, pp. 40–1.
[47]   For examples of Quaker and other Nonconformist businessmen see, in addition to works already cited, T. A. B. Corley, *Quaker Enterprise in Biscuits. Huntley and Palmers of Reading 1872–1972*, London 1972; A. E. Musson, *Enterprise in Soap and Chemicals. Joseph Crosfield and Sons 1815–1965*, Manchester 1965; Rhodes Boyson, *The Ashworth Cotton Enterprise. The Rise and Fall of a Family Firm 1818–1880*, Oxford 1970; D. A. Farnie, *John Rylands of Manchester*, Manchester 1993; W. P. Jolly, *Lord Leverhulme. A Biography*, London 1976; D. C. Coleman, *Courtaulds. An Economic and Social History*, Vol. 2, Oxford 1969; and articles in the *Dictionary of Business Biography*, ed. David Jeremy and Christine Shaw, 6 vols. London 1984–6.

CHAPTER TWO
Railways, Iron and Urban Development

Everything in South Durham and North Yorkshire dates from the making of the railway. In the beginning the Peases made the railway. Then they took to coal-mining to bring traffic to their railway. Then they made a new port to ship their coals; and the new port made a town which in thirty years became the capital of Cleveland, and the greatest iron-producing centre in the world. The railway created a demand for coke. They built coke-ovens by the hundred, and thus laid the foundations of a great and flourishing industry ... When a vast population was gathered together, in a district which had once but responded with the cry of the lapwing and the curlew's lonely note, members of the same family were ready to open out on the one hand a direct route to the Lake District, the tourist ground of England, and on the other to transform a sandbank and a smuggler's retreat into the watering places of Redcar and Saltburn ... [The Peases'] connection with the railway made them particularly alive to every want of the district through which it ran. They made the railway to serve the district, and then they developed the district to serve the railway.[1]

The writer of this tribute exaggerated the contribution of a single company and a single family to the development of south Durham and north-east Yorkshire; but there is no doubting the centrality of railways to the process nor the importance of the links between railways, coal and iron manufacturing. One facet of these links was the enterprises of the Pease family.

At the beginning of the nineteenth century the two principal towns of south Durham, Stockton and Darlington, were similar in size, market towns with a population of between 4000 and 5000, small compared with the commercial, shipping and industrial centres of Tyneside and Wearside. Stockton, at the highest navigable point on the river Tees, had iron and pottery manufactures, shipbuilding and shipping. Darlington, on the Great North Road, had industries related to the surrounding agriculture, linen and woollen manufacture and tanyards, and, as it turned out, better sources of capital. Not far away lay a part of the Durham coalfield which, compared with the well-developed northern part of the county, was handicapped by lack of access to a navigable waterway. Coal from the area round Bishop Auckland

[1]   *The Kings of British Commerce. The Peases of the North of England, Founders of the First Railway in the World*, n.p., n.d. [1876], pp. 27–8.

19

was sold over the south of the county and into north Yorkshire, but transport costs were high. It was assumed in the eighteenth century that land carriage doubled the pithead price of coal every ten miles. Anything that improved transport would be good for producers and markets.[2]

The idea of a canal to run from Stockton to Winston, higher up the Tees, to improve the district's transport facilities in general and reduce the cost of bringing coal from the Auckland field was first mooted in the 1760s; but the construction costs were high for a not very populous district, and the project lapsed for lack of interest. It was revived in 1812, now with a railway as a possible alternative. The eminent civil engineer John Rennie, commissioned to make a survey, was doubtful whether subscribers would get a return on their capital for many years. When discussion revived in 1818 it became clear that different groups had different ideas both about the line to be followed and about the form of transport. Christopher Tennant, an energetic merchant of Stockton, commissioned another survey for a canal from the Tees to the coalfield, running well to the north of Darlington. A further survey was commissioned by businessmen in Darlington and Yarm for a line from Stockton via Darlington to the coalfield, either a combination of canal and railway or a railway alone. George Overton produced plans for both alternatives, but recommended a railway all the way as the more efficient and economical. A public meeting at Darlington came down in favour of a railway over the entire route, convinced by the arguments of Edward Pease that it was the most efficient solution and a safe speculation. The banker Jonathan Backhouse, who had favoured a canal and was now converted to a railway, got rather carried away with his estimate of a 25% return on a capital investment of £120,000. Pease made no attempt to blind the meeting with figures but instead deliberately argued, on the basis of common sense and a fairly rough calculation from the tolls payable on the existing cart road from the Auckland field, that changing from rail to canal half way would damage the goods and increase costs, and that a return of 5% on the transport of coal alone was assured. 'This quite satisfied me,' he said. 'I am quite satisfied with my 5 per cent; and I have only made this statement to show that by one single article we can make a sufficient rate of interest by this undertaking, and all the

[2]   John Bailey, *General View of the Agriculture in the County of Durham with Observations on the Means of its Improvement. Drawn up for the Consideration of the Board of Agriculture and Internal Improvement*, London 1810, pp. 11–26, estimated the production of 35 land-sale collieries in central and south Durham as 390,000 tons of coal a year, as against 3.5 million tons from the sea coal mines of the Tyne and Wear area. Michael W. Flinn, *History of the British Coal Industry*, Vol. 2, Oxford 1984, pp. 18–24, 29–35, estimates the total production of the region in 1815 as 5,393,000 tons, and of sea sales as 2,988,000 tons. See also Robert Galloway, *Annals of Coal Mining and the Coal Trade*, Vol. 1, London 1898, pp. 72, 452.

rest may be taken as profits over and above 5 per cent.'[3]

Tennant did not succeed in raising capital for his project, but the subscription list for the Darlington scheme was closed at the end of the year, the majority of the shares being subscribed locally but substantial support coming from Quakers in London and the south of England. Two of these major subscribers were relatives as well as Friends: Thomas Richardson, partner in the bill-broking firm of Overend, Richardson and Gurney, was a first cousin of Edward Pease. Two of the daughters of Joseph Gurney of Norwich married respectively the younger Jonathan Backhouse and the younger Joseph Pease. The next stage was an act of Parliament, which would give the company power to purchase the land needed for the line. The proposed route of the railway crossed the estates of two of the most important landowners in the area, the Earl of Eldon, the Lord Chancellor, and the Earl of Darlington, later Marquis and then Duke of Cleveland. Eldon was bought off. Lord Darlington remained implacably opposed to a scheme which he described as 'a gross attack upon private property,' and 'harsh and oppressive, and injurious to the interests of the country through which it is intended that the railway shall pass,' and took his hostility so far as to try to bankrupt Backhouse's bank.[4] Lord Darlington was almost the only large landowner in the county who did not have industrial interests to balance against concern for his fox coverts. He and his eldest son remained for years obstacles to railway lines crossing their estates.

The first Stockton and Darlington Railway bill was defeated by thirteen votes in April 1819, but the proprietors were not discouraged. Overton was asked to make another survey with the object of avoiding Lord Darlington's property; other objectors were bought off; and a new act was applied for. A prospectus accompanying the bill talked exclusively in terms of local trade: 'General Merchandise will be carried from that Coast *upwards* and coal, Lime, Blue Stone for the repair of Roads and agricultural purposes *downwards*.' On a railway of this kind four horses could do the work that needed forty on the roads, so that 'By the facilities thus given to the conveyance the carriage will be reduced nearly *one-half* the present charge.' Traffic would be taken off the roads now 'infested' with carts and pack animals, and the demand on the

[3] *Durham County Advertiser*, 21 Nov. 1818. This account of the origins of the Stockton and Darlington Railway is based on William Weaver Tomlinson, *The North Eastern Railway: its Rise and Development*, Newcastle upon Tyne 1915, pp. 40–70; Kirby, *The Origins of Railway Enterprise*, pp. 26–35.

[4] Lord Darlington to Matthew Culley, 21 Apr. 1819, Northumberland Record Office, Culley Papers, ZCU 35; Lord Darlington to George Overton, 12 Jul. 1819, Newcastle upon Tyne City Library, Tomlinson Collection, Vol. 1; Maberley Phillips, *A History of Banks, Bankers and Banking in Northumberland, Durham and North Yorkshire*, London 1894, pp. 148–9.

agricultural interest for statute labour for the turnpikes would be reduced.[5] After intense lobbying, and a last-minute scare when it was found that the necessary percentage of the capital had not been subscribed, the shortfall could not be filled in London and Edward Pease supplied the extra £7000 needed, the first Stockton and Darlington Railway act was passed on 19 April 1821. The stated object was 'for making and maintaining a railway or tramroad from the River Tees at Stockton to Witton Park Colliery with several branches therefrom, all in the County of Durham,' with 'men and horses,' as the means of conveyance.

The role of horses was much reduced after Edward Pease met George Stephenson, now making a name as a railway engineer and pioneer of locomotives, and was converted by him to this still comparatively untried means of conveyance. After visiting Stephenson at Killingworth Pease wrote to Thomas Richardson that the more he saw of Stephenson the more impressed he was. The potential of locomotives fired Pease's normally sober imagination: 'Don't be surprised if I should tell thee there seems to us after careful consideration no difficulty of laying a railroad from London to Edinburgh on which waggons would travel and take the mail at the rate of 20 miles per hour, when this is accomplished steam vessels may be laid aside! We went along upon one of these engines conveying about 50 tons at the rate of 7 or 8 miles per hour, and if the same power had been applied to speed which was applied to drawing the waggons we should have gone 50 miles per hour – previous to seeing this locomotive engine I was at a loss to conceive how the engine could draw such a weight, without having a rack with teeth laid in the ground and wheels to work into the same or something like legs – but in this engine there is no such thing.'[6] Stephenson was appointed engineer to the line, and was asked to resurvey it and suggest improvements. One of these, offering easier gradients, would have taken the line farther away from Darlington. Edward Pease pointed out that it was Darlington that was putting up most of the capital, and Stephenson withdrew the suggestion.[7] Another act of 1823 allowed for steam power to be used for fixed engines in addition to locomotives, and now also the line was to be used for conveying passengers.[8]

---

[5] Stockton and Darlington Railway prospectus, DCRO D/XD/13/1.

[6] Edward Pease to Thomas Richardson, 10 Oct. 1821, DCRO, Hodgkin Papers, D/Ho/C 63/2. The meeting between Edward Pease and Stephenson passed into legend: Hunter Davies, *George Stephenson: a Biographical Study of the Father of the Railways*, London 1975, pp. 62–5.

[7] *History of the Darlington and Barnard Castle Railway, with Notices of the Stockton and Darlington, Clarence, West Hartlepool and other Railways and Companies in the District, by an Inhabitant of Barnard Castle* [Thompson Richardson], London 1877, p. 13.

[8] Tomlinson, *North Eastern Railway*, pp. 75–105; Kirby, *Origins of Railway Enterprise*, pp. 33–53.

After a number of financial vicissitudes but no major engineering difficulties the Stockton and Darlington Railway was formally opened on 27 September 1825. The proprietors assembled at the fixed engine at the foot of the incline at Brusselton, near West Auckland, 'and here the carriages, loaded with coals and merchandise, were drawn up the eastern ridge [from the Gaunless valley] a distance of 1,960 yards, in 7½ minutes, and then lowered down the plane on the east side of the hill, 880 yards, in 5 minutes.' The train of carriages, which now included a special covered coach for the proprietors and twenty-one waggons filled with passengers, as well as six coal waggons, was now attached to the steam locomotive and they set off for Darlington. 'Such was the velocity that, in some parts, the speed was frequently 12 miles an hour, and in one place, for a short distance, near Darlington, 15 miles an hour.' The journey from Brusselton to Stockton, a distance of just over twenty miles, took with stops a little over four hours. 'Throughout the whole distance, fields and lanes were covered with elegantly dressed females, and all description of spectators.' Where in one place the line ran close to the turnpike road, 'Numerous horses, carriages, gigs, carts and other vehicles travelled along with the engine ... without seeming in the least frightened'; and passengers on the train and on a stage coach had the opportunity to compare the power and speed of their respective conveyances. Francis Mewburn, the solicitor for the railway, 'never witnessed so great a crowd'; and by the time the cavalcade arrived at Stockton there were not fewer than 600 people on the train. The day ended with a dinner for the proprietors and their guests, and entertainment for the workmen.[9]

The promoters of the Stockton and Darlington Railway did not originally envisage shipping coal from the Tees: improving local supply, rather than competition with the Tyne and Wear in sea coal trade, was all they contemplated. By the time the railway was opened, however, Thomas Richardson had begun to explore the possibilities of a coastal trade in coal, and a Tees Coal Company was formed before the end of 1825. It soon became apparent that there was a substantial opportunity, and also that Stockton would not be able to handle a greatly expanded trade: the river was too shallow and too full of shoals for easy navigation despite recent and planned improvements. A better solution would be a port farther down stream adjacent to deeper water, and that would necessitate extending the railway.[10]

The Stockton and Darlington directors first considered Haverton Hill, on the north bank of the Tees, as a possible site for a port. It would have the

---

[9]   *Newcastle Courant*, 1 Oct. 1825; John Sykes, *Local Records, or Historical Register of Remarkable Events which have Occurred in Northumberland and Durham*, new edn. Newcastle upon Tyne 1833, pp. 187–9; Francis Mewburn, diary, 27 Sep., DCRO, D/XD/55/1.

[10] William Lillie, *The History of Middlesbrough. An Illustration of the Evolution of English Industry*, Middlesbrough 1968, p. 47.

advantage of serving also other proposals being devised by other groups for railways to bring coal from south-east Durham to the Tees or to Hartlepool, an old but decayed fishing harbour on the coast beyond the river mouth. The directors then decided in the autumn of 1827 to apply to Parliament for power to extend their line to Middlesbrough, a hamlet on the south bank of the river: its advantage over Haverton Hill was that the line would be shorter and, the river bank being less steep, loading would be easier. The decision for Middlesbrough caused a split among the proprietors of the railway. The Stockton group preferred Haverton Hill and resigned in protest against the Darlington Quaker domination of the company, reinforced as it now was by fresh Gurney money and parliamentary influence. The Middlesbrough bill was approved in May 1828, causing Joseph Pease to rejoice at 'the triumph over those who tho' hereditary British senators so far forgot their status as to oppose a measure fraught with public good for the sake of personal aggrandisement.'[11]

The choice of Middlesbrough was not inspired by Joseph Pease, as some stories have it, but he was an early supporter. In August 1828 he went to inspect the site along with some friends, taking a boat from Seaton Carew, a small seaside resort on the other shore, where he was spending the summer with his wife and two babies; 'and entering the Tees Mouth sail'd up to Middlesbro to take a view of the proposed termination of the contemplated extension of the Railway. Was much pleased with the place altogether. Its adaptation to the purpose far exceeded any expectation I had formed.' Apart from the farm house and a burial ground, and traces of other holdings, there was little to see; but 'Imagination here has ample scope in fancying a coming day when the bare fields we were then traversing will be covered with a busy multitude and numerous vessels crowding to these banks denote the busy seaport.' Joseph was cautious about very rapid development: 'Time however must roll many successive annual tides ere so important a change is effected, but who that has considered the nature and extent of British enterprise, commerce and industry will pretend to take his stand on this spot and pointing the finger of scorn at these visions, exclaim "That will never be"? If such a one appears he and I are at issue. I believe it will.'[12]

By the end of 1828 the Middlesbrough estate of 521 acres had been bought from its owner William Chilton, not by the Stockton and Darlington Railway proprietors but by a group of Friends – Thomas Richardson, Joseph Gurney, Henry Birkbeck, Simon Martin, and Francis Gibson (Edward Pease's son-in-law) – from London, Norwich and Saffron Walden, supported by non-Quaker London bankers. Joseph Pease, with his brother Edward,

[11]   Joseph Pease diary, 19 Oct. 1827, 5 Jan., 28 Apr., 13 May 1828, J. G. Pease Papers; Tomlinson, *North Eastern Railway*, pp. 172–3.

[12]   Joseph Pease diary, 18 Aug, 1828, J. G. Pease Papers, quoted in Lillie, *History of Middlesbrough*, p. 47; Kirby, *Men of Business*, p. 22, and elsewhere.

featured as one of the original Owners, but his one-fifth share of the £35,000 purchase price was lent to him by his father-in-law Joseph Gurney.[13] The railway extension was opened in December 1830.[14] By that time staiths for loading coal had been constructed and building of the town was beginning on 30 acres set aside on slightly rising ground near the river. 125 lots were auctioned, to tradesmen intending to set up businesses, and to Darlington investors such as Henry Pease who bought seventeen lots and Richard Otley, the surveyor who drew up the original plans and bought thirteen lots. The tradesmen included several builders, joiners and bricklayers who presumably intended to do much of the building work. A deed of covenant between the Owners of the estate and purchasers laid down the first local bye-laws. The Owners undertook to lay out and construct roads of a specified width, and to provide pavements, and sewers to carry off surface water, within four years. Houses fronting on the streets were to conform to certain standards of 'uniformity and respectability,' mostly of four rooms with a minimum height to the eaves, and minimum size of windows and doors. Occupiers were to sweep the pavements and provide spouts to carry off water from the roofs and drains under the footpaths. All were to do their best to prevent nuisances such as selling and slaughtering livestock anywhere but in the market or slaughter-houses, allowing ferocious dogs to roam unmuzzled or carts to obstruct narrow streets, dumping rubbish in the streets, leaving cellar doors uncovered at night without a warning light, letting off guns and fireworks, and playing football in the streets. Regular meetings of the Owners and occupiers would impose rates and elect a committee to manage the town. A surveyor would be employed to inspect the roads, superintend repairs, and collect the rates.[15]

Meanwhile the Stockton interests had resolved to back another railway, intended both to bring coal from the Coxhoe area to Haverton Hill and to join the Stockton and Darlington line at Simpasture and so gain access to the Auckland traffic. Despite opposition from the Stockton and Darlington company and from Lord Londonderry, who was beginning the construction of Seaham Harbour as a coal port for east Durham, what was now called the Clarence Railway was sanctioned in 1828, to run from Haverton Hill (later changed to Samphire Batts, renamed Port Clarence) to Simpasture. The

[13] Joseph Pease diary, 3, 10, 15 Dec. 1828, J. G. Pease Papers; H. G. Reid, ed., *Middlesbrough and Its Jubilee*, Middlesbrough 1881, p. 58; Owners of the Middlesbrough Estate title deeds Nos. 84–5, Cleveland County Archives, U/OME (2) 5.

[14] Tomlinson, *North Eastern Railway*, pp. 183–5.

[15] Deed of Covenant, 8 Feb, 1831, Cleveland County Archives, U/BSC 1/1; Lillie, *History of Middlesbrough*, pp. 49–52; Norman Moorsom, ed., *The Stockton and Darlington Railway. The Foundation of Middlesbrough*, Middlesbrough 1975, pp. 145–53; Norman Moorsom, *The Book of Middlesbrough*, Buckingham 1986, pp. 37–8.

promoters, however, had difficulty from the start in raising enough capital. Work did not start until 1830. Four years later about 28 miles of track had been brought into operation, but traffic was slow to develop and every obstacle was put in its way by the Stockton and Darlington Railway which, for example, by charging differential tolls on its line discouraged collieries in the Auckland area from sending coal for conveyance to Port Clarence. The Clarence company then tried to get direct access to the Auckland field by driving a tunnel through Lord Eldon's estate; but he resolutely refused permission for any line or tunnel, and financial difficulties obliged the company to hand over control to the Exchequer Loan Commissioners.[16]

Hartlepool was in many ways an obvious port for the coals of south-east Durham, but the harbour was at this time in a state of dilapidation. The inner harbour had been closed off by an embankment in the early years of the century, and the ground had been cultivated. Even after it was reopened, it had in 1833 only 3–4 feet of water at spring tides: at other times ridge and furrow could still be seen, 'save where the accumulated rubbish of centuries had piled up hills beyond the reach of the water.' The pier had been destroyed by a gale and was now a mere heap of loose stones.[17] But Christopher Tennant, leader of the Stockton group in the Stockton and Darlington Railway, settled in Hartlepool about 1830 and saw its potential as a coal shipping port. An act for improving the harbour was obtained in 1832, and another for a railway from east Durham. Engineering difficulties delayed work on the dock and the railway, but the first shipments were made in the summer of 1835.[18]

Neither the Hartlepool projects, nor various projects farther north, at this time involved the Stockton and Darlington Railway. But it was concerned with the movement that now began for linking London and Edinburgh. The earlier stages of this movement had to do with lines from York southwards, and were led by George Hudson, a draper of that city who became chairman of the York and North Midland Railway in 1833 and over the next fifteen years built up a remarkable empire. By speculative promotions and amalgamations Hudson largely created the 'railway mania' of the 1840s, but in the mid '30s his operations were still relatively modest.[19] As

16   Tomlinson, *North Eastern Railway*, pp. 161–90, 233–40. There was a lengthy dispute about charges between the Stockton and Darlington company and Jonathan Backhouse, owner of Black Boy colliery: it was eventually settled by arbitration. Public Record Office, RAIL 667/9. 1215.
17   William Tate, *A Description of these Highly Noted Watering-Places in the County of Durham, Hartlepool and Seaton Carew*, 2nd edn Stockton 1816, p. 7; Sir Cuthbert Sharp, *History of Hartlepool, with a Supplemental History to 1851 inclusive*, Hartlepool 1851, suppl. pp. 8–9.
18   Sharp, *History of Hartlepool*, suppl. pp. 4–23; Tomlinson, *North Eastern Railway*, pp. 207–29, 249–43.

far as lines north of York were concerned Joseph Pease proposed the Great North of England Railway to connect Leeds and York to Newcastle, using part of the Stockton and Darlington line. The Clarence Railway tried to get some of its line chosen for the route; but three eminent engineers, called in to adjudicate, came down in favour of the Pease proposal.[20] The bill for the Great North of England Railway came before Parliament in 1836. It was opposed by Tennant and the Stockton group, by some landowners who argued that a railway would spoil the privacy of their estates or who simply disliked the Darlington Quakers, and by the Duke of Northumberland who wanted to prevent the diversion of coal traffic from the waggonways on the Tyne in which he had an interest. Nevertheless the bill was passed, Joseph Pease playing an important part in Parliament. Henry Pease was among the first directors named, and the Stockton and Darlington Railway held shares.[21]

Two other projects in 1836 for lines to connect the Auckland area and Weardale with Hartlepool failed to get parliamentary approval; but in 1837 an agreement was reached between three groups to form the Great North of England, Clarence, and Hartlepool Junction Railway, to link Wingate to Byers Green and Hartlepool to Stockton. At the same time the Stockton and Darlington Railway decided to build a tunnel at Shildon which would cut out inclines and open up traffic from Crook. It also promoted a Bishop Auckland and Weardale Railway, to run as far as Witton. Joseph and Henry Pease were among the first directors named.[22]

By the summer of 1841 425 miles of railway line were open in the North East, more than half of them completed since 1835. There were 21 companies in operation, of which the Stockton and Darlington Railway was the most profitable. Already in 1827 it fulfilled Edward Pease's expectation of a 5% return on the capital, and the dividend rose to 6% in 1831 and 15% in 1841. A substantial proportion of the shares was now in the hands of the Pease family. Thomas Richardson, one of the original proprietors with 55 shares, held 141 by 1830, and in 1844 transferred all but 10 to John, Joseph and Henry Pease. These three also received the bulk of Edward Pease's shares and some from various Backhouses; so altogether between them they held 239 shares, almost a quarter of the total.[23] Only three other railways in the area, among them the

[19]   For Hudson see A. J. Peacock, *George Hudson 1800–1871. The Railway King*, York 1988–9.

[20]   Tomlinson, *North Eastern Railway*, pp. 272–82.

[21]   Francis Mewburn, *The Larchfield Diary. Extracts from the Diary of the Late Mr Mewburn, First Railway Solicitor*, Darlington 1876, pp. 43–4; Tomlinson, *North Eastern Railway*, pp. 285–6, 290–1; Kirby, *Origins of Railway Development*, pp. 124–5.

[22]   Tomlinson, *North Eastern Railway*, pp. 287–90, 297–300, 336, 348–9. Kirby, *Origins of Railway Development*, pp. 117–18.

[23]   M. C. Reed, *Investment in Railways in Britain 1820–1844. A Study in the*

Hartlepool Dock and Railway Company, gave a satisfactory return to the shareholders: the rest averaged only about 3.5%. All the lines were primarily engaged in carrying coal: passenger traffic developed only slowly. Down to the end of 1841 the Stockton and Darlington Railway had carried about 4.5 million tons, the Clarence Railway 1.5 million, the Hartlepool Dock and Railway Company about 2 million.[24]

Coal was shipped from Middlesbrough as soon as the railway was opened, and early in 1838 the Owners of the Middlesbrough Estate commissioned plans for a dock which was opened in May 1842. By 1845 the amount of coal shipped rose to over 500,000 tons.[25] Meanwhile the population grew from under 200 to over 5000, and further growth was expected. The town received a royal visit, from the Duke of Sussex, the Queen's uncle, in 1838. In 1841 a further step in municipal organisation was taken with an Improvement Act. Twelve commissioners, who must be substantial residents or ratepayers, were named: their successors were to be elected by the ratepayers. The commissioners were to have the sole management of all public streets, lighting and paving and the removal of rubbish. They were given power to construct common sewers, drains, wells and water pumps, to contract for gas supply (the Owners had set up a gas works in 1838), to provide markets and slaughterhouses, to provide fire engines (thatch was forbidden), and to compel the removal of nuisances. House owners were to be obliged to put up spouts to carry away water from roofs, and to repair ruinous houses.[26] In 1842 the commissioners recommended that owners should pave and drain the common yards of their property in the interest of public health, but this could not be enforced.[27]

The first improvement commissioners included some of the initial purchasers of plots in the town, and men who established a variety of industries, and also two close associates of Joseph Pease, William Fallows, harbour-master and shipping agent for the railway, and Isaac Sharp, agent for the Owners of the Middlesbrough estate. No member of the Pease family served on the improvement commission or, later, on the borough council. Joseph Pease acknowledged responsibility for the original plan of the town; he was instrumental in bringing industrialists to it; and he professed himself to be deeply interested in its welfare and progress. He paid the expenses of obtaining the first improvement act, and here as elsewhere he paid for the first

---

Development of the Capital Market, London 1975, p. 174.

[24] Tomlinson, *North Eastern Railway*, pp. 357–9, 364–8. Stockton and Darlington financial figures, Kirby, *Origins of Railway Enterprise*, pp. 127–32.

[25] John Walker Ord, *The History and Antiquities of Cleveland*, London 1846, pp. 533–40.

[26] 4 and 5 Vic. Cap. lxviii; Lillie, *History of Middlesbrough*, pp. 79–80.

[27] Improvement Commission minutes, 23 Dec. 1842, Cleveland County Archives, CB/M/C/1/1.

school and gave contributions to various chapels.[28] But despite their financial interest in the building and the communications of Middlesbrough, the Peases did not take a personal share in the affairs of the town in the way they did in Darlington: the improvement commission, and later the borough council, were left to others. One can only suppose that Joseph Pease and his brothers and sons, having no intention of living in Middlesbrough, preferred to keep their influence concentrated in Darlington.

The Owners of the Middlesbrough Estate, however, did influence the way the town developed, and they paid close attention to the estate's business. Some writers emphasise Joseph Pease's personal responsibility: one even asserts that in the early years the Owners exercised total control over every facet of town life and ran it politically.[29] It is difficult to find evidence of overt control. The 1831 covenant provided for annual meetings of the property owners, where the votes would indeed be weighted according to the value of the property but where the Owners of the estate could not have a majority. The deed went to great lengths to secure safe and orderly conditions in the streets, but did not try to regulate the conduct of business. No attempt was made, for example, to prevent the opening of public houses, as was done later in the Peases' mining villages. On the contrary, the 1841 census recorded four brewers, fifteen innkeepers (one of them an improvement commissioner), eighteen publicans and two spirit merchants living in the town and catering for a population of 5,500; and by 1859 there were said to be about eighty public houses and beershops as well as gin palaces.[30] Politically, only two of the twelve first improvement commissioners were directly connected with the Owners and the railway: the town council was at first dominated by the ironmasters and then by small businessmen and householders. The general direction in which the town developed was indeed to some extent determined by the owners of the land, and these by 1858 were all members of the Pease family. Land on the east and west sides of the estate was earmarked for industrial development: house building, initially confined to the area north of the railway, later expanded to the south. The net value of the estate was calculated in 1848 as £101,823 1s. 2d., nearly three times the original purchase price.[31]

[28] Reid, *Middlesbrough and its Jubilee*, pp. 144–7; Lillie, *History of Middlesbrough*, pp. 78–80; *South Durham and Cleveland Mercury*, 12 Feb. 1870.

[29] J. W. Leonard, 'Urban Development and Population Growth in Middlesbrough 1831–1871,' unpublished Ph.D. thesis, University of York 1976, pp. 55–6; Richard Lewis, 'The Evolution of a Political Culture. Middlesbrough 1850–1950,' in A. J. Pollard, ed., *Middlesbrough. Town and Community 1830–1950*, Stroud 1996, p. 105.

[30] M. J. Huggins, 'Leisure and sport in Middlesbrough, 1840–1914,' in Pollard, *Middlesbrough*, p. 147.

[31] Owners of the Middlesbrough Estate, valuation book 1844, account book 1848,

One of the first improvement commissioners was Henry Bolckow. He came to Middlesbrough in 1839 with his partner John Vaughan at the invitation of Joseph Pease, who offered them a site for a foundry and rolling mill. Bolckow, a German, had made a fortune as a merchant in Newcastle; Vaughan was an iron man; together they were looking for a place to develop a new enterprise. The works opened in 1841, at first using imported Scottish pig iron. Then in 1846 Bolckow and Vaughan began to use ironstone from Grosmont on the south side of the Cleveland hills, brought by sea from Whitby and sent up the Stockton and Darlington Railway to be smelted at their newly built blast furnace at Witton Park, and the pig iron brought back to Middlesbrough for fabrication.[32] The reason for building the partners' first blast furnace at Witton Park was the presence in that area of ironstone, which also supplied the Derwent Iron Company set up at Consett by Quaker Richardsons from Shotley Bridge and Sunderland. With enormous demand for iron rails in the railway boom of the mid 1840s, the Derwent Iron Company expanded rapidly; but the local ironstone, although plentiful, proved to be of poor quality and only worth using so long as it cost less than better ore brought from elsewhere.[33]

Joseph Pease was also instrumental in bringing to Middlesbrough from Kendal his cousin Isaac Wilson, who started a pottery and joined the engineering works of Gilkes, Wilkinson and Co. The Stockton and Darlington Railway leased the river dues from the Tees Navigation Company in 1845, and first leased and then took over the dock company. Joseph Pease advanced the money for the first lighted buoys in the channel below Middlesbrough.[34] All these activities added to the direct and indirect influence of the family and to the business of the railway company, which in 1851 carried about 75% of the coal shipped on the Tees; but they were a burden on the company's finances when trade was bad, as it was in the late 1840s.

In 1841 a struggle began over a direct route from Darlington to Newcastle, eight different companies being involved. The outcome was a victory for Hudson against the Stockton and Darlington company. Hudson

Cleveland County Archives, U/OME (2). 34, 49; Linda Polley, 'Housing the community, 1830–1914,' in Pollard, *Middlesbrough*, pp. 153–7.

[32] J. K. Harrison, 'The Production of Pig Iron in North East England 1577–1865,' in C. R. Hempstead, ed., *Cleveland Iron and Steel. Background and Nineteenth-Century History*, Redcar 1979, pp. 49–79. For Bolckow and Vaughan see J. S. Jeans, *Pioneers of the Cleveland Iron Trade*, Middlesbrough 1875, pp. 47–83; Reid, *Middlesbrough and its Jubilee*, pp. 113–41.

[33] Arthur Struthers Wilson, 'The Consett Iron Company Ltd, a case study in Victorian business history,' unpublished M.Phil. thesis, University of Durham 1973, ch. 1.

[34] *Report to the Lords Commissioners of the Admiralty by William Bald, Civil Engineer ... the Inspector appointed ... to make a Local Inquiry into the Case of the River Tees Conservancy Bill*, Parliamentary Papers, 1851, Vol. 29.

was building up his empire in the north of County Durham: in 1846 he got control of the Great North of England Railway, which changed its name to the York and Newcastle. Hudson paid over the odds for the company, and this became a factor in his downfall two years later; but meanwhile he bought up some local lines and the Sunderland docks (he became M.P. for Sunderland in 1845), and opened negotiations to take over the Hartlepool Dock and Railway company.[35]

The Stockton and Darlington Railway, however, although defeated over the Newcastle route, consolidated and strengthened its position in south Durham. The Shildon tunnel was opened in 1842. Further lines were opened, or leased, up the Wear valley from Witton to Frosterley, and from Crook to Consett. A line from Middlesbrough along the south bank of the Tees to Redcar, was also opened. These were at first separate companies, with Joseph and Henry Pease among their directors; but they all joined the Stockton and Darlington Railway in 1846–7.[36]

One project that still, however, eluded the inhabitants of south Durham was that for a railway to Barnard Castle. In 1832, on his first visit to the town to canvass for the parliamentary election, Joseph Pease was asked to promise support for a railway line. He did so, but nothing was done until 1844, when he accompanied a deputation from the town to Raby Castle. The Duke of Cleveland (son of the original opponent of the Stockton and Darlington Railway) 'courteously but very firmly refused to concur in any Railway near his property,' and remarked that 'Any reasonable man ought to be satisfied with having a railway station within 20 miles of him.' Joseph Pease, who had known the duke as an M.P. in the 1830s, was confirmed in the opinion that he was not a clever man, but narrow and prejudiced.[37] Faced with this resolute opposition the project had to be dropped for several years.

Meanwhile the new Stockton and Hartlepool company leased the lines of the Clarence railway, but it did not succeed in attracting the coal traffic it had anticipated: instead of carrying, as forecast to subscribers, 318,000 tons of coal a year, it only carried 195,000 tons in the first three years. For this lack of success it blamed the Hartlepool Dock and Railway Company, and the quarrel inspired Ralph Ward Jackson, a solicitor from Normanby practising in Stockton, to promote a new company. Fired by ambition to build something grand of his own, Jackson undertook the creation of a wholly new harbour and town on an empty site a little to the west of Hartlepool. In 1845

[35] Tomlinson, *North Eastern Railway*, pp. 453–60, 463–73; Kirby, *Origins of Railway Enterprise*, pp. 118–19.

[36] Tomlinson, *North Eastern Railway*, pp. 463–4, 473–5, 486; Kirby, *Origins of Railway Enterprise*, p. 120; T. E. Rounthwaite, *The Railways of Weardale*, London 1965; Lists of shareholders, 1847, DCRO, D/DL/23/11.

[37] Joseph Pease diary, 17 Oct, 1844, J. G. Pease Papers; Richardson, *Barnard Castle Railway*, pp. 24–7.

Hartlepool shipped 884,000 tons of coal as against Middlesbrough's figure of about 900,000 tons. In 1848, a year after the opening of West Hartlepool dock, the two Hartlepools together shipped over 1 million tons; and by 1850 the lead over Middlesbrough was large.[38]

The years 1847–9 were a period of general commercial crisis in Britain and Europe, accompanied by political upheaval, actual or threatened. The Stockton and Darlington Railway was badly affected by recession in the iron and coal industries. The leases it had undertaken at fixed rents became a heavy burden on shrunken revenue, and it had extended too much credit to some customers. The directors reported as early as 1846 continued depression in the coal trade, and in 1848 a year of unprecedented commercial difficulty. Over the next three years Edward Pease recorded in his diary losses of income and falls in the value of his shares. Joseph Pease, as treasurer of the Stockton and Darlington Railway, had to ask his father for an unlimited financial guarantee in 1847; but at the same time he came to the rescue of Bolckow Vaughan by standing surety for the firm in a banking panic. Joseph's diaries for these years record continuing anxiety, which began to affect his health.[39] In these difficult circumstances the railway's directors in 1848 proposed to lease the entire network to Hudson.

The downfall of Hudson, accused of share-rigging, selling his own shares to his companies at inflated prices, paying dividends out of capital, and false accounting amongst other forms of improper if not actually illegal behaviour, saved the Stockton and Darlington Railway from 'entanglement and disappointment.'[40] In the railway industry in general a new period of consolidation and amalgamation began. In 1850 the various companies operating north of York reached an agreement about sharing traffic, and in 1852

[38] For the creation of West Hartlepool see Major R. Martin, *Historical Notes and Personal Recollections of West Hartlepool and Its Founder*, West Hartlepool 1924, pp. 22–8; Robert Wood, *West Hartlepool. The Rise and Development of a Victorian New Town*, West Hartlepool 1967, pp. 39–49; Eric Waggott, *Jackson's Town. The Story of the Creation of West Hartlepool and the Success and Downfall of Its Founder, Ralph Ward Jackson*, Hartlepool 1980, pp. 1–9. For coal shipments see J. S. Jeans, *Jubilee Memorial of the Railway System. A History of the Stockton and Darlington Railway and a Record of its Results*, London 1875, pp. 174–80; R. W. Rennison, 'The Development of the North Eastern Coal Ports, 1815–1914: the Contribution of Engineering,' unpublished Ph.D. thesis, University of Newcastle upon Tyne 1987, Appendix B.

[39] Stockton and Darlington Railway, Management Committee reports to the Annual General Meeting, 1845–6, 1847–8, DCRO, D/XD/35/13, 16; *Diaries of Edward Pease*, pp. 230, 246–50, 275–6, 292, 294; Joseph Pease diaries, 1847, 1848, 1849, passim, J. G. Pease Papers; Tony Nicholson, '"Jacky" and the Jubilee: Middlesbrough's Creation Myth,' in Pollard, *Middlesbrough*, p. 40.

[40] Management Committee report, 1848–9, DCRO, D/XD/35/16. For Hudson's fall see Peacock, *George Hudson*, chs. 23–5.

negotiations began which led to the formation two years later of the North Eastern Railway.[41] But this company, although controlling the communications from Leeds and York to Edinburgh, did not control communications between the Tees, south Durham, and Cumberland.

These now took on increased importance with the opening up of the main seam of the Cleveland ironstone at Eston on the north side of the Cleveland hills near to the Tees estuary. The existence of the seam had been known since 1812, but its depth and purity were not appreciated until John Vaughan and his mining engineer investigated an outcrop in 1850. Bolckow and Vaughan took out a mineral lease and built a private branch railway to join the Middlesbrough to Redcar line near Grangetown. They then built a blast furnace at Eston Junction. By 1856 other companies had also taken out leases; and production from all the mines totalled over one million tons, of which Eston accounted for nearly half. Some of the ironstone was sent up to Witton Park and Consett for smelting, some was smelted in the thirty blast furnaces established within a six-mile radius of Middlesbrough – Middlesbrough itself, South Bank and Cargo Fleet, Stockton, Port Clarence, Ormesby and Darlington.[42]

The Peases were involved directly and indirectly in a number of these enterprises. They were not very successful at picking mining sites, but later took over the Derwent Iron Company's royalty at Upleatham and Hutton Lowcross. In iron-making, the South Durham Ironworks at Darlington had Henry Pease as chairman; directors of Gilkes Wilson Leatham and Co. at Cargo Fleet included Quaker relatives (Charles Leatham was married to Joseph Pease's daughter Rachel; Isaac Wilson was a cousin and his daughter married John Beaumont Pease). Other firms had connections with the Stockton and Darlington railway.

All of this activity was of immediate benefit to the railway, carrying ironstone up to Witton Park and Consett and the pig iron back to Middlesbrough, and now increasingly carrying coal from south Durham and limestone from Weardale to the blast furnaces around Middlesbrough. The railway's mineral traffic increased from 1,433,695 tons in 1850 to 2,478,870 tons in 1855. Despite their heavy financial obligations Joseph Pease and his eldest son Joseph Whitwell took personal responsibility for a new branch line from Middlesbrough to Guisborough, which opened in 1853; and the Stockton and Darlington Railway planned further expansion in the Crook and Auckland area and contemplated buying the Clarence Railway.[43] The

---

[41] Tomlinson, *North Eastern Railway*, pp. 493–505, 515–19.

[42] J. S. Owen, 'The Cleveland Ironstone Mining Industry'; J. K. Harrison, 'The Production of Pig Iron in North East England 1577–1865,' in Hempstead, *Cleveland Iron and Steel*; Kirby, *Origins of Railway Enterprise*, pp. 147–8.

[43] Tomlinson, *North Eastern Railway*, pp. 507–09, 523–4; William Fordyce, *A History of Coal, Coke, Coalfields ... Iron, its Ores, and Processes*, Newcastle upon

project of a railway to Barnard Castle was also revived, only to meet the continued adamant opposition of the Duke of Cleveland. Local promoters argued that a railway would bring benefits to the town and suggested that the duke was indifferent to its welfare. He replied listing the benefactions he had made to the town and the welfare of the poor and the aged, and went on: 'I will not disguise that I have always had the greatest aversion to having my property cut up by railroads, and I believe, as a landowner, that I am not singular in that respect. I am perfectly ready, however, to allow that all trunk lines are essential for the public good, and must be submitted to; with branch lines, however, it is very different, they are almost all vicious in principle, and ought to be resisted as more detrimental than advantageous to the district; but wherever they are permitted, it ought to be from the landowners taking the initiative, and from being the promoters, to be the principal shareholders themselves.' The railways built in the district so far had been built on inferior land, but 'the valley of the Tees between Barnard Castle and Darlington, which may be called the garden of Eden, as regards the county of Durham, has always been kept sacred, as never intended to be desecrated by the formation of a railroad, and which, as far as I am concerned, shall never take place with my consent.' The duke now said, however, that he would not object to a line that had been proposed, that ran to the west of Raby Park.[44]

This other line was proposed by Ralph Ward Jackson, whose rivalry with the Stockton and Darlington Railway took on a strongly personal note. While the Stockton and Darlington company was considering buying the Clarence Railway in 1851 Jackson stepped in and secured a perpetual lease of the Clarence line from the Stockton and Hartlepool Railway and then amalgamated it with his own Hartlepool West Harbour and Dock company. The combined firm was now entitled the West Hartlepool Harbour and Railway Company.[45] As far as Barnard Castle was concerned, Jackson proposed a line from Bishop Auckland, which did cross the Raby estate but to the west of the park. Two bills were put forward to Parliament. Joseph Pease was examined at length over the Darlington to Barnard Castle one: Jackson's opposition to it was a personal attack. The Darlington bill was lost, but Jackson's bill was also defeated. Eventually a second Darlington to Barnard Castle bill was passed in 1854 and the line was opened in 1856. Henry Pease was among the first directors.[46]

Tyne 1860, p. 144; Kirby, *Origins of Railway Enterprise*, p. 154.

[44] Duke of Cleveland to promoters of Barnard Castle railway, 17 Mar. 1853, Newcastle upon Tyne City Library, Tomlinson Collection, Vol. 1; Richardson, *Barnard Castle Railway*, pp. 45–53.

[45] Martin, *Historical Notes*, pp. 29–39.

[46] House of Commons, Evidence, 1853, Vols. 72–3, Darlington and Barnard Castle Railway Bill; Evidence, 1854, Vols. 44–5, Barnard Castle and Bishop Auckland Junction Railway and Branch Bill, Darlington and Barnard Castle Railway;

The development of iron-making had a dramatic effect on the town of Middlesbrough. Its population more than doubled in the 1850s, rising to 18,992 in 1861. Some infilling of the original plan had already taken place by 1853, the town was beginning to spread, and newspaper reports refer to 'building mania.'[47] By 1856 all the land originally earmarked for housing had been disposed of, and land south of the railway was being sold. Like other towns Middlesbrough was visited by cholera in these years, the last outbreak in 1853-4 being the worst. The sanitary condition of the town was the subject of a report to the General Board of Health soon afterwards. The inspector, William Ranger, considered the town's water supply adequate; but the poorer houses did not have water laid on, tenants could not afford to lay pipes, property owners were often unwilling to do so, and the new municipal corporation (the town received a charter of incorporation in 1853) did not have power to compel them. The sewers were 'wholly inadequate,' but the corporation was doing something about them and the Owners of the Middlesbrough Estate were willing to bear part of the cost. Privies were in the middle of yards and courts. The streets were wide, but had been laid out in the first instance without proper regard for health. The overriding problem was overcrowding. 'Middlesbrough is an instance of a town springing into existence in the course of a few years, and increasing in population and commercial importance with almost unexampled rapidity; consequently building sites have been scarce, and the value of land proportionately increased. Naturally, under such circumstances each house builder has made it his chief care to put together as many houses as possible on the smallest space.' The Owners of the Middlesbrough Estate sold the building sites and did not or could not control what was built. The existing legal powers were insufficient, and must be amended. 'There would be no objection to the present fashion of building the houses of the labouring population in courts, if the space in the centre were large enough, and the means of through ventilation provided. But as these courts are now arranged, with other houses built behind them, and the entrance merely by a narrow passage through one of the houses, it is impossible for the occupants to get a breath of pure wholesome air. The corporation are carrying out a plan of main sewerage, and it is to be hoped, that as it progresses, more general cleanliness and better accommodation will be provided throughout the town. But even when all that can be done, has been done in these most important respects, most of the courts described in my personal inspection of the district will remain close, ill ventilated, and consequently unwholesome places of abode. These faulty arrangements must and will prevail till the law puts a stop to them. As long as there are more people seeking houses than there are houses to be obtained; in

---

Richardson, *Barnard Castle Railway*, pp. 54-8; Tomlinson, *North Eastern Railway*, pp. 509-10, 523-4; Kirby, *Origins of Railway Enterprise*, pp. 158-60.

[47] Leonard, 'Urban Development and Population Growth,' pp. 103-16.

other words, as long as the demand exceeds the supply, so long will builders and owners endeavour to supply the deficiency by providing defective house accommodation.'[48]

This is a sorry picture of a town little more than twenty years old and initially laid out on a plan with specifications on such matters as width of streets and height of buildings, doors and windows. What had gone wrong? Although the plan had been departed from already before the rapid population growth began in the early 1850s, there can be little doubt that this growth was the chief cause of the overcrowding: with such a manifest need for quick housing, it could not be expected, as Ranger said, that builders would not put up as many houses as possible on each plot, or that landlords would not fill them with as many tenants as possible. The question mostly is how far in the circumstances of the time, the law, and the place, overcrowding, bad building and bad sanitation could have been prevented. The 1831 covenant exemplifies prevailing attitudes to property and public health. It went into great detail about the use and misuse of streets, which were public space, but apart from prescribing the external appearance of houses fronting on the streets it said nothing about building standards or occupancy of private property. Twenty years later, attitudes were beginning to change. In the second half of the 1850s, no doubt as a result of Ranger's report, the Owners of the Middlesbrough Estate required buyers of land for house building to provide house and yard drains to connect with the sewers, to provide a water closet and ash pit for each house, to supply water, and not to allow cellars to be used as dwellings. In 1856 a select committee of the House of Commons, considering a bill to extend the town's boundaries, was told that the Owners of the Middlesbrough Estate sold the land freehold and had not built the houses: Joseph Pease, however, owned 800 houses and leased several hundred more. He admitted to the committee that mistakes had been made in the original layout of the town; but he said the conditions he had laid down had been subverted, and he agreed with Ranger that new legislation was needed to enable standards to be enforced. The improvement commissioners seem to have done quite well since 1841 on such matters as draining and lighting the streets and preventing nuisances; but they did not have powers over building standards or domestic drains. John Dunning, surveyor for the new local board of health and formerly agent for the Owners of the Middlesbrough Estate, emphasised to the select committee the need for quick housing; but he thought the Owners, who were after all operating in a seller's market, had not exercised as much control over what was built as they could have done, and

[48] *Report to the General Board of Health on a Preliminary Inquiry into the Sewerage, Drainage, and Supply of Water, and the Sanitary Condition of the Inhabitants of the Borough of Middlesbrough, in the North Riding of the County of York. By W. Ranger Esq.*, London 1854. Ranger's emphasis on ventilation suggests that he believed in the miasma theory of the spread of infection.

might earlier have imposed conditions on purchasers such as they had now adopted.[49]

There are not many examples of early Victorian planned towns with which to compare Middlesbrough. West Hartlepool equally grew from almost nothing – the township of Stranton, in which the new town was situated, had a population of 381 in 1831 – to some 4000 in 1851 and 21,000 in 1871. It seems to have been less planned than Middlesbrough, but more under the control of one man. The land was owned by Jackson's West Harbour and Dock company; he laid out one wide street intended for public buildings and a church, and streets of working-class houses laid out on a grid plan were built by the early 1860s. An improvement act was obtained in 1854, and the town was run by commissioners dominated by Jackson until it became a borough in 1887. There was no local board of health. The town was never inspected for the General Board of Health; but there is little reason to suppose that it would have fared better than Middlesbrough.[50] The only real contemporary or near contemporary English case of a whole planned town is Saltaire near Bradford, but its nature – a company town built by a single wealthy individual – was so different from that of Middlesbrough that comparison is not very useful.

The new Act gave Middlesbrough borough council power to lay down standards for housing but did not oblige it to do so: until bye-laws were adopted in 1868 development was hardly better regulated than it had been in the early 1850s. Population continued to grow fast, quadrupling between 1851 and 1871 and nearly doubling again by 1881. By selling land for building the Owners of the Middlesbrough Estate were able to influence the direction in which the town spread, southwards from the line of the railway; but they seem to have responded to demand rather than having any strategic plan. Nor were they alone in the market: during the 1860s a neighbouring landowner, Thomas Hustler, sold land to the north-east of the Estate for housing and industrial development. The Estate itself sold on average 4½–5 acres a year for housing between 1853 and 1868. The forty houses they allowed to the acre were less than the density allowed by the borough council, but were still obviously very cramped.[51] The demand was for housing near the iron works. As Florence Bell, wife of the ironmaster Sir Hugh Bell wrote in her account

[49]   House of Commons, Evidence, 1856, Vol. 34, Select Committee on Middlesbrough Extension and Improvement Bill; Owners of the Middlesbrough Estate, land sales agreements, Cleveland County Archives, U/OME (2) 5/1; Leonard, 'Urban Development and Population Growth,' pp. 140–93; Lillie, History of Middlesbrough, p. 159.

[50]   Martin, Historical Notes, pp. 25–6, 54–7, 62–3; Wood, West Hartlepool, pp. 42–9, 87–96; Waggott, Jackson's Town, pp. 2–9, 16–83.

[51]   Owners of the Middlesbrough Estate, valuation book 1868, Cleveland County Archives, U/OME (2) 4/35; Polley, in Pollard, Middlesbrough, pp. 157–63; Lillie, History of Middlesbrough, pp. 404–05.

of Middlesbrough shortly before the First World War: 'The workmen all struggle to be as near as possible to their work, to waste no time or money in transit.'[52] In 1875 a new Public Health Act, giving all local authorities power to regulate the construction of new buildings, marked a change in attitudes to government intervention and ushered in, in Middlesbrough as elsewhere, a new period of municipal activity.

The principal benefactor of Middlesbrough was Henry Bolckow. He gave the town its first public park in 1868, and schools with accommodation for 900 children. He subscribed to every local good cause, and left generous bequests in his will. He was the first mayor, and the first M.P. when Middlesbrough became a parliamentary constituency in 1868, having to be naturalised as a British subject for the purpose. He was president of the chamber of commerce and chairman of the Middlesbrough Exchange Company. The benefactions of the Pease family were substantial but not outstanding. The Owners of the Estate gave the land for the first Church of England church to be built, in 1838; in 1856 they provided the first school and replaced it with new buildings in 1870. The Owners gave land for Middlesbrough High School in 1875, and members of the Pease family served on its board of trustees for many years. Other gifts included land for a cemetery. Joseph Whitwell Pease gave the town a fire engine.[53]

Railway development in the area in the 1850s was bound up with Cleveland ironstone. More and more royalties were being let and more railways projected. The Stockton and Darlington and its associates engaged in an increasingly bitter struggle with Ralph Ward Jackson's West Hartlepool company. This company proposed a line from the south bank of the Tees opposite Port Clarence (to which waggons would be transported by ferry) round by a long loop to Brotton. The Stockton and Darlington company objected, and fought back by surveying another line. Joseph Pease also tried to block the proposed ferry by applying to the Crown for a lease of the whole foreshore of the Normanby estate. The Tees Navigation Company, set up in 1808, had been giving increasing grounds for dissatisfaction. It was perpetually short of money, and had done practically nothing to improve navigation downstream from Cargo Fleet. In 1851 the Stockton and Darlington Railway forced its hand by presenting a bill to take it over. The result was a new Act setting up the Tees Conservancy Commission, with members appointed by local authorities and by the Admiralty. Joseph Pease was one of the latter, and four other members were connected with the Stockton and Darlington Railway. The Commissioners now presented a bill that would allow the imposition of new tolls on ferries, and would transfer their powers to the

[52]   Lady (Florence) Bell, *At the Works. A Study of a Manufacturing Town*, London 1907, pp. 2–4.
[53]   *South Durham and Cleveland Mercury*, 12 Feb. 1870; J. W. Pease diary, 5 Feb. 1870, 3 Aug. 1875, J. G. Pease Papers.

railway company.[54]

The company was now planning extensions at both ends of its network. At the western end it was not a matter of tourism in the Lake District, whatever the author of *The Kings of British Commerce* said, but of improving the supply of haematite iron ore from Cumberland. Hitherto the ore had been brought to the Derwent Iron Company by the Newcastle and Carlisle railway and up to Consett by a series of rope inclines, while the Cleveland ironstone was brought by inclines from Crook. In 1856 a bill was obtained for a railway from Stocksfield on the Tyne to near Consett: at the same time the North Eastern Railway projected a line to Consett up the Lanchester valley west of Durham.[55] More ambitiously the Stockton and Darlington company planned a new trans-Pennine line via Barnard Castle over to Kirby Stephen and Tebay. Henry Pease was a moving spirit, and one of the first directors of the South Durham and Lancashire Union Railway, approved by Parliament in 1857. The crossing of Stainmoor, a considerable feat of engineering, was completed in 1861.[56]

Even when the local ironstone proved inferior, the Derwent Iron Company enjoyed the vital asset of abundant cheap local coking coal, and limestone nearby. By 1858 it was leasing 3,000 acres of local coal royalties and working four pits and 543 coke ovens. It had eighteen blast furnaces, and produced 150,000 tons of manufactured iron.[57] But the company never made a profit, either because it was inefficient or because it was very heavily indebted to the Northumberland and Durham District Bank which had financed much of its growth. Not long after the trans-Pennine railway line was approved the bank failed, having lent far too much money on inadequate security, including £1 million to the Derwent Iron Company. Newcastle Quakers were involved in both the bank and the iron company. The latter had been founded by Quakers; the former incorporated the Newcastle, South Shields and Sunderland branches of Backhouses bank and its managing director, Jonathan Richardson, was a Quaker and former Backhouses manager. The monthly meeting investigated the responsibility of six iron company shareholders, who acknowledged a lack of vigilance; but Jonathan Richardson refused to cooperate. He was disowned, and several members of his family then resigned.[58] Closure of the Derwent Iron Company would have been so serious

---

54 *Report to the Lords Commissioners of the Admiralty [on] ... the River Tees Conservancy Bill*, Parliamentary Papers, 1851, Vol. 29; Tomlinson, *North Eastern Railway*, pp. 551, 563–8; Lillie, *History of Middlesbrough*, pp. 53–4. 121–2.

55 Tomlinson, *North Eastern Railway*, pp. 558–9, 562.

56 Tomlinson, *North Eastern Railway*, pp. 558–63, 596–7.

57 Wilson, 'Consett Iron Company,' ch. 1; Tomlinson, *North Eastern Railway*, p. 562.

58 Ruth Sansbury, *Beyond the Blew Stone. 300 Years of Quakers in Newcastle*, Newcastle upon Tyne 1998, pp. 175–9; Phillips, *History of Banks*, pp. 340–5.

for a number of local interests, including the railways, that after a couple of abortive attempts at buy-outs a new company was set up in 1864, with broad ownership including the bank's creditors and the public, and the railway companies suspended charges for two years. David Dale, who had started his career as a protégé of the Peases, became managing director of the new Consett Iron Company.[59]

Meanwhile in Cleveland competition over railways in the ironstone district reached new heights. In May 1858 several bills were before Parliament. In addition to two railway companies, a number of other interests were involved – the town of Stockton, still opposed to anything that favoured Darlington; the town of Middlesbrough; the Tees Conservancy Commission; various landowners; and the lessees of different royalties. The enquiry into the bills was marked by Ralph Ward Jackson's hostility to Joseph Pease. In his evidence to the House of Commons select committee Jackson hinted very strongly that Joseph Pease aimed to monopolise the entire ironstone traffic for the benefit of his own interests, and accused the Stockton and Darlington Railway of trying to prevent coal merchants in Middlesbrough from getting supplies by the West Hartlepool system. Joseph Whitwell Pease pointed out in reply that for the railway to put obstacles in its customers' way would be commercial suicide. Eventually Parliament approved the construction of a line from Guisborough to Skinningrove by a company partly owned by the West Hartlepool Harbour and Railway Company; but transporting the ore from the south bank of the Tees still depended on the Stockton and Darlington Railway since the act did not sanction a ferry and the House of Lords refused the new Cleveland Railway Company additional power to ship the ironstone to the Tyne or overseas. The Stockton and Darlington Railway offered improved rail facilities via Middlesbrough, and with the other hand tried to prevent the Cleveland company having access to the river by again claiming the foreshore of the Normanby estate at Cargo Fleet. In this it was unsuccessful, but its friends the Tees Conservancy Commissioner tried physically to stop Jackson building a jetty. Jackson engaged men to remove the Commissioners' obstructions and a pitched battle took place, in which at least one man was seriously injured.[60]

Jackson was victorious over the jetty, but by this time the West Hartlepool Harbour and Railway Company was in difficulties. A disgruntled debenture-holder, Benjamin Coleman, who had a personal financial dispute with Jackson's brother, mounted a campaign for an enquiry. A 'committee of

---

59 Wilson, 'Consett Iron Company,' ch. 2; Consett Iron Company Ltd., List of Allotees [1864]; Kirby, *Men of Business*, pp. 39–40.

60 House of Commons, Evidence, 1858, vols. 18–19, Select Committee on Durham and Cleveland Union Railway bill; Evidence, 1859, Vol. 12, Select Committee on Cleveland Railway bill; Martin, *Historical Notes*, pp. 42–4; Tomlinson, *North Eastern Railway*, pp. 568, 570–4.

assistance' was appointed in 1859, but its report was a whitewash. Coleman continued his campaign, petitioning against a bill that would allow the company to raise new capital. Eventually a new enquiry on behalf of the debenture-holders found that the company had spent nearly £1 million more than the authorised share and loan capital, its excess borrowing totalled £2.4 million, and there was only £14,000 in the revenue account to meet interest due of £168,000. Ships had been bought, and inducements given to shipping companies to use the port, without legal authority. Jackson was forced to resign but remained unrepentant, continuing to justify his actions. He remained influential in West Hartlepool and was elected its M.P. in 1868.[61] Jackson was not personally dishonest: there was no question of fraud, and unlike Hudson he did not make very large personal gains. He was a man of great ambition and vision, reckless and given to self-deception, exceeding, in pursuit of his vision, the legal limits on his company and the bounds of financial prudence, and carrying his fellow directors with him for much longer than they ought to have followed.

Jackson's fall led to the reorganisation of the West Hartlepool Harbour and Dock Company, and in 1865 it merged with the North Eastern Railway. By this time an even more important amalgamation had taken place, Negotiations between the North Eastern Railway and the Stockton and Darlington Railway began at the end of 1859 in a friendly atmosphere. The chief aim of the Stockton and Darlington delegation, led by John Pease and Joseph Whitwell Pease, was to secure local control over its network. In view of the way the network had been built up, its success, and the Peases' stake both in it and in the industries that supplied much of its traffic, it was not an unreasonable aim. The settlement reached provided for a special 'Darlington Committee' which would manage the Stockton and Darlington network for ten years with the possibility of an extension. Two North Eastern directors would sit on the committee, three Stockton and Darlington directors would sit on the board of the North Eastern Railway. The financial arrangements were also favourable. Stockton and Darlington shareholders were guaranted a 15.25% share of the joint receipts and a price of £225 for every £100 of stock held.

At this point four members of the Pease family – Joseph, his brothers John and Henry, and his son Joseph Whitwell – between them held 19,624 shares, valued at £299,410. Henry Pease was the only member of the Stockton and Darlington board to vote against the merger in March 1860. He had been the chief strategist of the railway in the 1850s, so his appointment as chairman of the Darlington Committee when the amalgamation went through was an appropriate recognition of his services as well as, presumably, soothing to his

---

61   Waggott, *Jackson's Town*, pp. 109–38; Tomlinson, *North Eastern Railway*, pp. 599–603, 610–11.

feelings.[62]

After the amalgamation the Pease family's relations with the railway were less personal but still important. They remained large shareholders, and in 1870 when the capital of the two companies was consolidated they received £136 worth of North Eastern Railway stock for every £100 of Stockton and Darlington Railway stock. Henry Pease remained chairman of the Darlington Committee until it came to an end in 1879. He, and Joseph Whitwell sat on the board of the North Eastern Railway from 1863; Joseph Whitwell became chairman in 1894. And in September 1875 Henry, the only surviving member of the founding generation, presided over the celebrations for the jubilee of the Stockton and Darlington Railway. These took place in Darlington, with processions, a banquet in a specially constructed marquee, an exhibition of locomotives, publication of celebratory articles in the press, works such as J. S. Jeans's *Jubilee Memorial of the Railway System* (a complimentary copy of which was given to every guest at the banquet), and the unveiling of a statue of Joseph Pease. This act was performed by the fourth Duke of Cleveland, who as Lord Harry Vane had been M.P. for South Durham between 1841 and 1859, rose above his father's and his eldest brother's dislike of railways and of Peases, and did what might have been an embarrassing task in a 'straightforward and courageous' way.[63]

As a North Eastern Railway director Joseph Whitwell Pease was a useful spokesman for the railway interest in Parliament in the 1870s and 80s. He served, along with other prominent directors, on select committees on railways in 1881–2, 1891, and 1893, concerned with railway rates, safety, and working hours. All were opposed to increased regulation. In the 1881–2 committee the seven railway directors voted as a bloc: later the companies were less united, and became divided in their political allegiance. In the 1890s the North Eastern Railway was more moderate than other companies about rates and about collective bargaining with the trade unions.[64] In this the company mirrored the Pease attitude in the coal industry. Equally, Sir Joseph's position on employers' liability reflected his colliery as well as his railway interests. In a debate on a bill put forward in 1876 to abolish the doctrine of common employment, which made it impossible for a man to sue his employer in respect of injuries if any fellow worker was even remotely responsible for the accident, Sir Joseph did not express outright opposition but wanted the doctrine better defined. He pointed out that all the leading railway companies supported insurance schemes to which the men

[62] Tomlinson, *North Eastern Railway*, pp. 585–7; Kirby, *Men of Business*, pp. 41–2; Kirby, *Origins of Railway Enterprise*, pp. 167–73; 'Stockton and Darlington Railway, shares 1862,' Nuffield College, Gainford Papers,13.

[63] *Northern Echo*, 28 Sep. 1875; *Durham Chronicle*, 1 Oct.; Jeans, *Jubilee Memorial*, pp. 304–15.

[64] Geoffrey Alderman, *The Railway Interest*, Leicester 1973, *passim*.

contributed and which covered all accidents however caused. Morally, if not legally, he said, 'the liability was acknowledged by the masters in their contributions to these institutions'; but they might well not continue to contribute if they were also to be made liable for a narrower class of claim that would not discourage carelessness. That bill failed, but efforts continued. In another debate in 1880 Sir Joseph moved an amendment to support insurance schemes, which he maintained were a better way to cover all accidents. The Employers' Liability Bill of 1880 did not prohibit companies requiring men to join their schemes and to contract out of the act's provisions.[65]

North East England, and specifically Cleveland, provided a vastly growing share of enormously expanding iron production after 1850.[66] The reason for Cleveland's increasing dominance was that to produce a ton of pig iron required a greater weight of ironstone than of coke: it was cheaper to bring the coke to the ore than the ore to the coke, although Consett continued to do it the other way round until its end. The great expansion in iron-making therefore took place very largely on Teesside, near to the Cleveland ironstone and convenient for exporting the products by sea and, later, importing ore from Spain and North Africa. Five new works were opened between 1855 and 1865.[67] The area was relatively slow to take to steel production, partly because of its dominance in iron-making and partly because the local ore was not suitable for steel-making until the development of the Thomas-Gilchrist process.[68]

The Peases, although connected with a number of the local firms and substantial shareholders in Wilsons Pease and Co. and the South Durham Ironworks, were not ironmasters. They became, however, large-scale ironstone producers, from mines at Upleatham (taken over from the Derwent Iron Company), Hutton Lowcross, Loftus, Craggs Hall and Lingdale. The output of the mines in 1873 was 1.2 million tons (over 29% of the total for the area). Over 2000 men were employed. By the mid-70s J. W. Pease and Co. was the largest producer of ironstone in Cleveland.[69] Unlike the colliery owners the ironstone mine lessees did not on the whole build villages for their

65   *The Parliamentary Debates*, 3rd ser., vol. 229, cols. 1172–7; vol. 255, cols. 574–9; Alderman, *Railway Interest*, pp. 64, 74–5. See also below, p. 60.
66   Alan Birch, *The Economic History of the British Iron and Steel Industry 1784–1879*, London 1967, pp. 124–5, 128, 135–6.
67   Harrison, in Hempstead, *Cleveland Iron and Steel*, pp. 49–79.
68   J. S. Carr and W. Taplin, *History of the British Steel Industry*, Oxford 1962, pp. 83–7, 94–7.
69   Fordyce, *History of Coal*, pp. 142, 144; Northern Echo, *The Durham Thirteen. Biographical Sketches of Members of Parliament returned from the City, Borough and County of Durham in the General Election of 1874*, Darlington 1874, pp. 153–4; Reid, *Middlesbrough and its Jubilee*, p. 104; Jeans, *Pioneers of the Cleveland Iron Trade*, pp. 139–40; J. S. Owen in Hempstead, *Cleveland Iron and Steel*, pp. 33–4.

workers but left provision to speculative builders. Joseph Pease did not exactly plan the miners' villages at New Marske, Hutton Lowcross, Lingdale and Skinningrove, but they seem to have benefited from his interest and to have been better to live in than most. Everywhere he provided a school and a chapel, and often a mechanics' institute: the one at Hutton Lowcross started as early as 1858; a new one was opened at New Marske in 1876.[70] In 1864 Joseph Whitwell Pease gave evidence to an enquiry into the conditions of miners other than coal miners. He said that there was no hospital at Hutton Lowcross and Upleatham, but there was one at Marske, which he had finished and to which Lord Zetland (owner of the Upleatham royalty) subscribed. There were two ambulances and the men were willing to go to the hospital. There was a doctor, paid for by the company, and both it and the men contributed to a scheme that included medical attendance on families. The scheme paid sums of money to men who were off work sick or suffering from minor accidents. All the houses were four-roomed, two up and two down, with gardens large enough to keep a pig. Some of the men owned their own houses, some rented them; and already, after furnishing their houses to their own taste, the men, who had mostly come from working as navvies on the railways, were settling down as denizens. They were in general steady and orderly: the one policeman in Marske, provided for by the company and Lord Zetland, was underemployed. There was a school and a new reading room, and a school at Guisborough where about half the Hutton miners lived. There was a penny savings bank and some of the men subscribed to building societies, 'but as a class. I should not say they are very saving.' The company employed a visiting missionary who had a good influence.[71] The one amenity the Peases did not provide in their villages was a public house. In ironstone mining, as in the colliery villages, the Peases did their best to promote temperance.

The Peases were remembered with respect and affection by elderly mineworkers in later years, but less so by competitors.[72] Although Joseph Whitwell and his family lived at Hutton Hall, only a few miles from the mines, they do not seem to have visited them more often than they did the collieries. Personal involvement with employees seems to have been confined to those directly connected with the family.

[70] Durham Chronicle, 22 Nov. 1861; B. J. D. Harrison, 'Ironmasters and ironworkers,' in Hempstead, Cleveland Iron and Steel, pp. 231–53, esp. 235–6; Ena L. Halloway and Alan Hughes, New Marske Looking Back, New Marske 1982..

[71] Commissioners Appointed to Inquire into the Condition of all Mines to which the Provisions of the Act of 23 and 24 Vic. C.151 do not apply. Report, together with Appendix, Parliamentary Papers, 1864, Vol. XXIV, pp. 384–9.

[72] Owen in Hempstead, Cleveland Iron and Steel, p. 34.

CHAPTER THREE
Coal

In March 1819 a south Durham clergyman informed a neighbouring landowner whose property was affected by the proposed Stockton and Darlington railway, that the 'scheming, artful and deceitful' Quakers, especially the Backhouses, were buying collieries in the area in order to profit from the expected business.[1] The Backhouses were among the first in the field, acquiring Black Boy colliery near Shildon. The Peases were not far behind, starting in 1827 when Joseph Pease leased his first coal properties near Bishop Auckland.[2] Adelaide colliery was opened in 1830, followed by St Helen Auckland, Eldon and Tindale. Then, a few miles to the north, came Roddymoor near Crook, which expanded into the complex of Peases West comprising nine pits – Job's Hill, Bowden Close, West Emma, West Lucy, West Edward, Wooley, Sunniside, and Brandon, and associated coke works. There was also Windlestone near Ferryhill; and later expansion over the hill from Crook to Esh and the Deerness valley, Hedleyhope, Waterhouses and finally Ushaw Moor. Already in 1859 the colliery branch of the family businesses was the largest single source of Joseph Pease's income. In the 1870s and 1880s the combined output of these collieries was not less than one million tons of coal a year, about one third of it converted to coke for the iron industry. In 1884 four thousand men and boys were employed. In the 1890s Pease and Partners were the third largest colliery firm in the North East and among the top ten or twenty nationally.[3]

The Peases' colliery business expanded in the context of an enormous overall expansion of the industry. Production rose nationally from some 32 million tons a year in the early 1830s to 271 million tons just before the First

[1] Rev. Thomas Peacock, Denton, to Matthew Culley, 7 Mar. 1819, Northumberland Record Office, Culley Papers, ZCU 35.
[2] Joseph Pease diary, 28 Oct., 30 Oct., 1 Nov., 10 Dec. 1827, J. G. Pease Papers; T. H. Hair, *A Series of Views of the Collieries in the Counties of Northumberland and Durham*, London 1844, pp. 47–50.
[3] Roy Church, *History of the British Coal Industry*, Vol. 3, Oxford 1986, pp. 126, 397, 402, 404; Jeans, *Pioneers of the Cleveland Iron Trade*, pp. 129–48; *Fortunes Made in Business. A Series of Original Sketches, Biographical and Anecdotal, from the Recent History of Industry and Commerce, by Various Writers*, London 1884, pp. 331–79; Fordyce, *History of Coal*, p. 98; Kirby, *Men of Business*, p. 43.

World War: the rise in the North East was from some 7.1 million to 54.2 million tons.[4] The Pease business was located in the part of the Durham coalfield that, unlike the Tyne and Wear area, had not been highly developed before the railway opened it up to new investment. The Peases joined an industry where the men who leased colliery land, opened and worked the pits, were no longer landowners using their own resources including agricultural rents, but men, still mostly of local origin, whose capital came from trade, railway development, and other industry. By 1830 only a minority of landowners in the North East were still working their collieries themselves; but two of those who did, the Earl of Durham and the Marquis of Londonderry, remained among the very largest producers until the end of the century. The growing scale of enterprises and the initial costs of sinking and winning a new pit varied widely according to geological conditions, averaging perhaps £20,000 to £30,000 in 1829 and £50,000 to £80,000 in the early 1850s. Edward and Joseph Pease and four other partners put £40,000 into the St Helen Auckland colliery.[5]

The enormous expansion of the coal industry required equally large expansion of the labour force and, especially in the hitherto thinly populated area of south-west Durham, the provision of housing and at least some of the requirements of social life. The Peases did not manage their coal-related enterprises themselves, employing professional managers instead. The ups and down of the coal trade were largely beyond their control. But as Quakers they were concerned with social questions, and they can be shown to have been more active than many of their fellow colliery owners in various forms of social provision in the area that their enterprises dominated. This chapter will be largely concerned with the social aspects.

The population of the area grew rapidly. The township of Crook and Billy Row, for example, the site of Peases West, had 228 inhabitants in 1821, 538 in 1841, then took off to 9401 in 1871 and over 11,000 at the end of the century. New recruits, obviously necessary at a time of rapid expansion, seem mostly to have been drawn from a fairly limited area. Men moved around within the coalfield, but there is not much hard evidence about inward migration from farther afield, except for Irish and others brought in to break a strike in 1844, and later some miners from Cornwall whose occupation at home had come to an end. There was very little recruitment of boys from outside the industry: miners married the daughters of miners, sons followed their fathers into the pits.[6] The isolated villages that were often thought of as

4   Church, *British Coal Industry*, Vol, 3, pp. 2–3, 189.
5   House of Lords, *Select Committee on the Coal Trade*, Sessional Papers, 1829, Vol. 8, pp. 45, 50; J. R. Leifchild, *Our Coal and Our Coal Pits. The People in Them and the Scenes around Them*, London 1853, pp. 121–3; Valuation of St Helen Auckland colliery, Tyne and Wear Archives, Wilson of Forest Hall Collection, DF/WF, 28/1, George Johnson Report Book No. 2, pp. 208, 223.

the standard mining settlement, and of which south-west Durham had a large share, were obviously single-occupation settlements, but even on the Tyne and Wear, where miners lived in or near towns alongside other workers, pitmen appeared to observers to be a race apart.

This 'race' was commonly characterised, at the time and later, as uncouth, intemperate and thoughtless, living in overcrowded hovels and spending every penny earned. The pitmen were 'a rude, bold, savage set of beings, apparently cut off from their fellow men in their interests and feelings.' They lacked 'that civilization which binds the wide and ramified society of a great city ... The pitmen have the air of a primitive race.' The colliers were 'not ill-natured, ill-disposed or criminal.'[7] Indeed there was much evidence of 'the simple-minded, good-natured and harmless character of the colliers, and of their gratitude to those who treat them with kindness. On the other hand ... they are migratory and unsettled, and are thus brought much less under the influence of persons of superior rank than those whose employment is more continuous ... The mode of life of the colliers is reckless, improvident, and coarse. They often earn high wages, with short hours, and where this is the case they spend their money not merely in intemperance of the usual kind, but in the strange and almost unmeaning extravagance, with which sailors in former times squandered their prize-money.'[8]

But there was also much evidence of an improvement in manners and morals. In 1834 a local writer was quoted as saying: 'Amidst all their dangers, the pitmen are a cheerful, industrious race of men. They were a few years ago much addicted to gambling, cock-fighting, horse-racing, etc. Their spare hours are directed now to a widely different channel; they are for the most part members of the Wesleyan sects; and, not infrequently in passing their humble but neat dwellings, instead of brawls and fights you hear a peaceful congregation of worshippers uttering their simple prayers, or the loud hymns of praise breaking the silence of the eventide.'[9] Thomas Wilson, miner turned teacher, clerk, popular poet and town councillor in Gateshead, wrote in 1843: 'The pitman is no longer the same ignorant, degraded being that his forefathers were. This important change may be attributed to the following causes: first, the establishment of Sunday schools for the purpose of teaching the children to read; secondly, the general diffusion of useful knowledge in

6   Church, *British Coal Industry*, Vol. 3, pp. 25–34, 615–20. For the stereotype of the mining settlement see John Benson, *British Coal Miners in the Nineteenth Century. A Social History*, Dublin 1980, pp. 1–5, 81–8.

7   Aeneas Mackenzie and Metcalf Ross, *An Historical, Topographical and Descriptive View of the County Palatine of Durham*, Newcastle upon Tyne 1834, pp. cxiv–cxvi.

8   Privy Council, *Report of the Commissioners appointed to Inquire into the State of Popular Education in England* [Newcastle Commission], London 1861, Vol. 1, pp. 214–17, also Vol. 2, p. 323.

9   Mackenzie and Ross, *Historical ... View*, pp. xv–xvi.

cheap publications; and thirdly, the introduction of Savings Banks.' Forty years earlier, 'it was no unusual thing to see whole families of young men spending the Sunday in gambling and idleness. Now, on the contrary, such a thing is rarely to be seen; for in passing the doors of neat cottages, we frequently find the inmates reading; or, if absent, they will be either in the Methodist chapel or a prayer-meeting; and, instead of appearing in the very meanest clothing, and not infrequently in rags, we now see them not only clean and well dressed, but civil and very orderly.'[10] One of the commissioners sent to enquire into the employment of children in mines and factories reported of south Durham that 'Both men and boys on Sundays are dressed exceedingly well. The men generally wear a black suit, and a stranger seeing them would hardly suspect them to be the men whom he had seen coming up from the pits begrimed with sweat and coal dust, and as black as negroes. Some of the witnesses in evidence, and all persons in conversation, give the credit to the Wesleyan Methodists of having brought about a great change in the respectability of dress and general good behaviour of the miners.' A witness told the commissioner, Dr Mitchell, that three quarters of the pitmen at Pease's Deanery and Adelaide collieries attended a place of worship, and there was a Sunday school attached to every such place.[11]

On the whole, miners enjoyed a reputation for hard drinking and improvident spending down to the end of the century: in 1891 mining counties and seaports had the highest rates in the country for proceedings for drunkenness offences.[12] But the effect of religious conversion on the lives of those who experienced it is thoroughly attested, and great importance was attached to religion in bringing about improvement. Whether the spiritual agents were Wesleyan or Primitive Methodists, or other sects or the established church, religious provision in the colliery districts was a concern for the churches and for employers. In County Durham the Church of England was handicapped by a medieval parochial geography which bore little relation to the facts of population growth and changes in distribution. To take one example, the ancient parish of Brancepeth, a few miles south-west of Durham, with an area of over 20,000 acres, included six (later seven) townships. In 1841 for the first time the total population reached 2000: in 1851 Crook and Billy Row alone had more inhabitants than the whole parish ten years earlier. And while Brancepeth village itself remained about the same size (between 400 and 500 inhabitants) for most of the century, Crook and Billy Row, Brandon and Byshottles, Helmington Row, Tudhoe amd Willington grew by factors of twenty, thirty, or sixty. In 1891 the combined

[10]   Thomas Wilson, *The Pitman's Pay and other Poems*, Gateshead 1843, pp. vii–viii.
[11]   *Commission for Inquiring into the Employment and Condition of Children in Mines and Manufactories*, Parliamentary Papers 1842, Vol. 15, para. 705; Vol 16, pp. 150–1.
[12]   Harrison, *Drink and the Victorians*, p. 315.

townships had a population of 44,472. The church at Brancepeth was not in the centre of the parish. To reach it the people of Crook and Hedleyhope had a walk of about six miles, those from Willington and Tudhoe about four. To meet the new conditions Crook was made a parish of its own, with a church completed in 1845. Willington got a chapel of ease in 1857 and became a parish in the 1870s, as did Tudhoe and Brandon. Similar developments took place all over the diocese of Durham: altogether 102 new parishes were established between 1862 and 1898, and 119 new buildings were started.

As for other denominations, altogether well over 100 chapels, two thirds of them Methodist (Wesleyan and Primitive in approximately equal numbers), and fourteen Roman Catholic churches, were built, mainly by the efforts of the congregations concerned, in the colliery districts of the county between 1830 and 1890.[13] The Peases only rarely gave money to Anglican church building. To non-Anglican churches and chapels they subscribed, gave land, and laid foundation stones, for example at Ushaw Moor, Waterhouses, Hamsterley, Crook, Cockfield, Shildon, Spennymoor and West Auckland. In this generosity they can be compared with their fellow colliery owner Joseph Love, who as a devout New Connexion Methodist gave handsomely to his own denomination but would not encourage any other chapels in his colliery villages. The Marquis of Londonderry, whilst mostly supporting the established church and, for example, building a church at his new development at Seaham Harbour, also gave materials and a subscription to Methodist chapels at Pittington and Broomside. The Peases employed a missionary at Peases West to conduct Scripture readings and encourage 'habits of temperance and order among the Colliers and their families.'[14]

Religious provision and education were inseparable in the minds of contemporaries, and are difficult to separate for historians. Thomas Wilson attributed the improvement he observed in the manners of miners in the first place to the opening of Sunday schools to teach the children to read. No

---

[13] *Kelly's Directory of Durham*, London 1890.

[14] John Pease, Darlington, to Josiah Forster, Tottenham, 6 Jun. 1853, DCRO, Hodgkin Papers, D/Ho/ C 52/89; *Durham Chronicle*, 5 Aug. 1859, 22 Sep. 1871, 10 May 1878, 25 Jul., 1879, 22 Apr. 1887; J. A. Pease to J. W. Pease, 23 Apr. 1888, 21 Feb. 1892, Ruskin College, Oxford, Gainford Papers, 3,4. Pease and Partners, and Sir Joseph Pease personally, contributed to the enlargement of the Baptist chapel at Waterhouses in 1901: *Durham Chronicle*, 11 May 1901. See Robert Moore, *Pit-men, Preachers and Politics. The Effects of Methodism in a Durham Mining Community*, Cambridge 1974, p. 70; Norman Emery, 'Pease and Partners and the Deerness Valley,' unpublished MA thesis, University of Durham, 1984, pp. 63–5. For Love see J. Y. E. Seeley, 'Coal mining villages of Northumberland and Durham. A Study of Sanitary Conditions and Social Facilities 1870–1889,' unpublished MA thesis, University of Newcastle upon Tyne 1973, p. 226; E. Welbourne, *Miners' Unions of Northumberland and Durham*, Cambridge 1923, pp. 115–16. For Pittington see DCRO, Londonderry Papers, D/Lo/B 256(49).

doubt a good deal had been done on Tyneside by the 1840s, but reports on south Durham, whilst noting that the Methodists, both Wesleyan and Primitive, were widely praised for their efforts at Sunday schools, said that the standard of teaching was low and the effect limited. Three boys at Black Boy colliery may serve as an example. The eldest, George Green, aged 16, said that he went to the endowed school at Bishop Auckland until he started work in the pit at 11, and used to go to Sunday school. He had learned the catechism but did not understand it, he could say the Lord's Prayer but had forgotten the creed and the Ten Commandments. He sometimes read the Bible but never a newspaper. George's brother John, aged 11, went to a Sunday school at the local Independent chapel. He could read but not write, could say the Lord's Prayer but not the Ten Commandments. Another boy of 10 sometimes went to Sunday school but could not read and did not know the Lord's Prayer or the Ten Commandments.[15]

Some promoters of the Sunday school movement had only been concerned with religious education and were doubtful, for example, whether children should be taught to write. By the 1830s, however, the provision of general elementary education for working-class children had become a matter of national concern. The government began to give grants to two school societies, the National Society (an Anglican body) and the British and Foreign School Society (a non-denominational Protestant body). A parliamentary select committee reported in 1838, however, that the provision of elementary education was 'lamentably deficient,' that what there was reached only a small proportion of those who ought to receive it, and that without strenuous efforts on the part of government, great social evils were likely to follow.[16]

Eighty-six new schools were founded in the North East coalfield between 1820 and 1844, and the strike of the latter year seems to have given some additional impetus. Lord Londonderry was said in 1846 to be spending £300 a year on schools; and two thirds of the children at three of his villages were now at school. Enquiries round Bishop Auckland showed that existing schools were being expanded. Joseph Pease had promoted the establishment of a British school at St Helen Auckland; one had existed at Black Boy colliery for about three years; there were good schools at Consett, Witton Park and Tow Law.[17]

[15]   *Commission for Inquiring into the Employment and Condition of Children in Mines, Reports from Sub-Commissioners*, Parliamentary Papers 1842, Vol. 16, pp. 143–4, 159–61.

[16]   *Report of the Select Committee on the Education of the Poorer Classes in England and Wales*, Parliamentary Papers 1837–8, Vol. 7, pp. 165–6. For the Sunday school movement see W. R. Ward, *Religion and Society in England, 1790–1850*, London 1972, pp. 12–16, 135–41; John Ferguson, ed., *Christianity, Society and Education*, London 1981.

[17]   *Report of the Commissioner Appointed, Under the Provisions of the Act 5 & 6 Vict., c.*

Provision of school buildings and teachers was not enough to ensure that children attended for long enough to profit. Setting a lower age limit on boys starting work was a contentious issue. In 1842 Lord Ashley's Mines Act prohibited the employment of women and very young children underground. Women had never been so employed in the North East, but there was a good deal of concern about the short-term effect of banning boys under 10, and in practice there was widespread evasion through collusion between employers and workers. Joseph Lawson, Joseph Pease's colliery agent, and Thomas Cockin, the manager of Pease's Deanery colliery, told the sub-commissioner enquiring into the employment of children that it would be a relief to the owners if the age limit were made 9, and they themselves could manage without boys under 12; but other collieries could not, and the workers would object. The North East viewers (mining engineers) as a group agreed that if boys were not initiated into the pits before they were 13 or 14 they could never become colliers. Nor could the pitmen possibly afford to keep their children at school until they were 16.[18] One possible answer was to induce boys to attend school part time after they started work. Seymour Tremenheere, the commissioner who reported annually on conditions in the mining districts, recommended that boys between 10 and 14 should attend school for not less than 300 hours per year, attendance being recorded by the school and checked by the colliery manager. The Earl of Durham's manager had told him that 'Notwithstanding the number of good schools which for some years have existed in the colliery villages ... the boys very seldom remain long enough at them to learn anything that is much use to them ... It would be attended with excellent effects if they were obliged to go to school for a certain portion of their time for some years after they commence work.' If this were done, by the time the boys were 14 'they would have learned to read with some ease and pleasure, and the master would be able to put good books into their hands from our lending libraries.'[19] In the next two years Tremenheere found general support among North East miners for the idea

99, to *Inquire into the Operation of that Act, and into the State of the Population of the Mining Districts* (these reports are henceforth cited as *Mining Commissioner's Report*, with year), Parliamentary Papers 1847, Vol. 24, pp. 13–30; *Durham Chronicle*, 28 May 1846; Abstract showing the number of children being educated at Londonderry schools, DCRO, Londonderry Papers, D/Lo/B 312. See also Robert Colls, '"Oh Happy English Children!" Coal, Class and Education in the North East', in *Past and Present*, 73 (1976), pp. 75–99; A. J. Heesom and Brendan Duffy, 'Debate. Coal, Class and Education in the North East, in *Past and Present*, 90(1981), pp. 136–51,

[18] *Commission for ... Inquiring into the Employment of Children in Mining, Sub-Commission Reports*, Parliamentary Papers 1842, Vol. 16, pp. 124–5, 150–1; J. Buddle to H. Lambton, 28 May 1842, DCRO, National Coal Board Papers, Buddle Collection, NCB 1/JB/1786.

[19] *Mining Commissioner's Report*, Parliamentary Papers 1852–3, Vol. 40, pp. 775–7.

that boys should work only half the day underground and spend the other half at school; but provision for half-time schooling had to wait until the Mines Regulation Act of 1872 prohibited the full-time employment of boys under 12, and laid it down that between the ages of 10 and 13 boys should attend school half time.[20]

The Newcastle Commission found that colliery owners were the chief providers of schools in their areas and the clergy were apparently less interested in education. It was said that 'where the land is chiefly in the hands of the clergy, capitalists employing labour underground are thwarted and hindered in their exertions for progress; and that this accounts for the backward state of the schools in the mining parts of Weardale and Durham [Poor Law] Unions, while the greater freedom of Auckland in this respect combined with the enterprising philanthropy of its leading coalowners is the reason for the generally superior state of the schools ... Almost all the coalowners ... do something towards the maintenance of schools, and are anxious that education should be a true cultivation of the intellectual and moral powers of the children.' The clergy professed to agree, but were almost universally regarded as an obstacle to progress.[21] Outside the coalfield, up Weardale and Teesdale, the London Lead Company (a Quaker firm) and the Beaumont Lead Company had a good record in school provision; and their example inspired Shute Barrington, Bishop of Durham from 1791 to 1826, to found schools in the same area.[22] Most of the colliery schools, as the Newcastle Commission said, were provided by the colliery owners. The Earl of Durham had paid for three by 1841; the Marquis of Londonderry was responsible for ten, attended by 1500 children, on his colliery estates by 1858; Messrs Straker and Love built schools at Oakenshaw, Brandon and Willington; Bell Brothers paid for schools at Page Bank and Tursdale. Some owners were more energetic and personally interested than others. Lord Londonderry, for example, received regular reports on 'his' schools, but there is no record of personal involvement.[23] The Peases, on the other hand, were assiduous in visiting and opening the schools they helped to pay for and whose teachers' salaries they underwrote.

[20] *Mining Commissioner's Report*, Parliamentary Papers 1854, Vol. 19, pp. 611–12; 1855, Vol. 15, pp. 555–6; 1856, Vol. 18, pp. 566–7, 575–7.

[21] Privy Council, *Report ... into the State of Popular Education*, Vol. 2, pp. 335, 343–5.

[22] Ray Pallister, 'Educational Investment by Industrialists in the Early Part of the Nineteenth Century in County Durham,' in *Durham University Journal*, 61 (1968–9), pp. 32–8.

[23] Reports on Schools at Penshaw, Rainton, Pittington and Old Durham, 1858, 1861, DCRO, Londonderry Papers, D/Lo/E 516, 517; A. J. Heesom, 'Entrepreneurial Paternalism: the Third Lord Londonderry (1778–1854) and the Coal Trade,' in *Durham University Journal*, 66 (1974), esp. pp. 247–9; *Report into the State of Popular Education*, Vol. 2, pp. 327, 335; Emery, 'Pease and Partners and the Deerness Valley,' pp. 156–7.

As Quakers the Peases could not approve of church control of education nor support church schools. Before they arrived on the scene there already existed Quaker-founded schools at Shildon, Shotton and Bishop Auckland. These were supported, the Shildon one being rebuilt at Joseph Pease's expense. For new schools the British and Foreign School Society provided the answer. Joseph Pease helped to set up a British school at Bishop Auckland before 1846. In the 1850s and 60s Joseph Pease and his son Joseph Whitwell were laying the foundation stones and visiting schools at Peases West, Waskerley, Waterhouses and Bowden Close, and contributing to the Roman Catholic parochial school at Crook.[24] Crook presented a problem of disputed control. The school there was built in the 1830s by the efforts of the local freeholders and ratepayers, and in 1849 Joseph Pease and the proprietors of Peases West built a schoolmaster's house. The Church of England incumbent then claimed the title to the school. A committee of investigation in 1860 found in favour of the ratepayers, but the vicar refused to accept the verdict. Eventually, after unsuccessfully lobbying the bishop, Joseph Pease cut the Gordian knot by organising the establishment of a British school next door, paid for by his company and other local colliery owners. He laid the foundation stone in February 1866 and the school opened a year later. With the population continuing to grow, a new Board school was needed at Crook in 1877: its foundation stone was laid by Arthur Pease.[25] In 1871 it was the turn of Esh, where a temporary iron building was opened to meet the needs of fifty children while a permanent school was built. In 1874 a new school was opened at Esh Winning, and in the following year Joseph Whitwell Pease opened one at Stanley Crook. This was intended to accommodate 250 children, with 150 more in a projected infant school.[26]

Efforts were also made at adult education. A mechanics' institute was opened at Crook in 1851, and Joseph Pease and Partners contributed to two subsequent enlargements. Joseph Pease personally provided money for lectures at Peases West and Crook, and a travelling library to serve reading rooms at all his collieries: the writer of an article in the *Newcastle Weekly Chronicle* noted that the reading room at Shildon was one of those which the Peases 'appear to think as necessary an appendage to a colliery as is the pump, or the ventilator, or the hauling apparatus. They seek to elevate their men as

---

[24] *Mining Commissioner's Report*, Parliamentary papers 1846, Vol. 24, pp. 404–05; J. W. Pease diaries, 8 Jan., 26 May 1856, 30 Jan. 1864, J. G. Pease Papers; *Durham Chronicle*, 15 May 1863, 5 Feb. 1864; William Fordyce, *The History and Antiquities of the County Palatine of Durham*, Newcastle upon Tyne 1857, Vol. 1, pp. 439–40; Jeans, *Jubilee Memorial of the Railway System*, pp. 243–5.

[25] *Darlington and Stockton Times*, 17 Mar. 1849; *Durham Chronicle*, 7 Sep. 1860, 26 Jan. 1866, 1 Mar. 1867, 20 Jul. 1877; *Northern Echo*, 7 Feb. 1872.

[26] J. W. Pease diary, 18 Nov, 1871, J. G. Pease Papers; *Durham Chronicle*, 14 Aug. 1874, 15 Jan. 1875.

well as their coals.' The British school at Crook was opened for the use of clubs in the town, and evening classes for young men were projected.[27] In speeches at foundation-stone laying and school opening ceremonies Joseph Pease and his sons spoke of the blessings of education in equipping young people not only with the ability to read and write and communicate ideas, but also with spiritual values and the capacity to make decisions about their lives. But it was difficult to get boys and young men to come to night school. Joseph Whitwell Pease, giving evidence to a parliamentary select committee on coal in 1873, whilst taking pleasure in the fact that attendance at the schools in his district had gone up by about 25% in the last five years, admitted that the evening schools he had tried to establish had failed, mainly because earlier elementary schooling had been inadequate. 'A man to whom reading and writing are difficult has no pleasure after a day's work in going into an evening school'; 'A night school is a hardship to a person who cannot read and write easily.'[28]

The stereotype of colliery housing is one of rows of back-to-back terraced cottages in dreary isolated villages. The reality was always more varied, with numbers of miners at all times living in towns alongside other workers. But colliery villages, large and small, were standard in County Durham, especially in the parts newly developing in the nineteenth century. Here the colliery owners built houses, at first out of necessity to attract labour to what were sometimes remote parts, and then as a means of retaining men. Rents were mostly deducted from wages. Some companies in the North East provided houses rent free to hewers, and eviction was used as a weapon against strikers. This practice declined later in the century as a greater variety of housing became available; but it was still used, for example, at Ushaw Moor (not then a Pease and Partners colliery) in 1882.[29] In villages that served more than a single colliery the houses might be built by a variety of providers. The North East had the highest proportion in the country of miners living in company houses.[30] Towards the end of the century owner-occupation increased, as did private building for rent and co-operative society building; but still as late as 1904 the mining engineer Henry Armstrong was advising Pease and Partners to build some 150 new houses at Windlestone and Eldon.[31]

[27] *Durham Chronicle*, 26 Sep. 1851, 4 May, 10 Aug. 1860, 1 Mar., 18 Oct. 1867, 24 Nov. 1871; *Newcastle Weekly Chronicle*, 31 May 1871; A. E. Pease journal, 3 Oct. 1887, J. G. Pease Papers.

[28] *Report from the Select Committee on Coal*, Parliamentary Papers 1873, Vol. 10, pp. 152–67.

[29] *Durham Chronicle*, 6 Jan. 1882; H. Diana Brown, 'Colliery Cottages 1830–1915. The Great Northern Coalfield', in *Archaeologia Aeliana*, 5th ser. 23 (1995), pp. 291–305..

[30] Church, *British Coal Industry*, Vol. 3, pp. 277–81, 599–601.

[31] Benson, *British Coalminers*, pp. 107–10; Edward Lloyd, *The Story of Fifty Years of*

The early houses were probably of a quality comparable with those of agricultural labourers. Sketches and estimates for new cottages at Byers Green and Roddymoor in the 1840s show two-roomed houses, one up and one down, the attic room unceiled and low at the sides, with a floor area of about 18' x 16' and a small back pantry, costing between £5 and £11 10s. to build.[32] Standards rose from the middle of the century, but in 1859 Tremenheere reported that 'Although many of the principal proprietors of collieries have of late years expended large sums of money in improving the old kind of houses, and in building new ones on a better model ... rows of houses are still being built, back to back, or with restricted space between them and without any provision whatever for decent habits and the means of cleanliness.' Such houses were said to have cost between £40 and £50 each to build. Another £10 to £20 each would bring them up to a usual standard: the men could afford the extra rent and a ground of complaint would be removed.[33]

An investigator in 1861 described the colliery villages for the most part as 'miserable and repulsive': the houses at Ushaw Moor from which strikers were evicted in 1882 were described in a local newspaper as 'the most wretched dwellings it is possible to conceive.'[34] But inside bad houses could often be found comfortable furniture and household goods. The work was hard, dangerous and often uncertain, but hewers, at least, could earn good wages. One observer, writing in 1835, said that most of the old pitmen, and many of the younger ones, had a taste for expensive furniture, and 'it would be impossible for a stranger to pass in front of the lowly dwellings, three or four hundred in number, adjacent to Jarrow colliery, for example, without being struck by the succession of carved mahogany bedposts, and tall chests of drawers, as well as chairs of the same costly material, which are presented at almost every open door.' Another writer commented in 1853 on the contrast between the 'confined and dismal' cottages and the 'comparatively showy and costly' furniture, an eight-day clock, a good chest of drawers and 'a fine four-post bedstead – the last two often of mahogany, and sometimes of a very superior kind.'[35] Joseph Whitwell Pease told the Select Committee on Coal in

    Crook Co-operative Society, Pelaw 1916, pp. 193–4; J. W. White and R. Simpson, *Jubilee History of the West Stanley Co-operative Society Ltd 1876 to 1926*, Pelaw 1926, pp. 68–72, 224; Thomas Ross and Andrew Stoddart, *Jubilee History of the Annfield Plain Industrial Co-operative Society 1870 to 1920*, Manchester 1921, pp. 92–3; H. Armstrong to Pease and Partners, 19 Apr, 1904, Northumberland Record Office, Armstrong Collection, NRO 725/B 14/547 ff.

[32] Northumberland Record Office, North East Institute of Mining Engineers Archives, Watson Collection, NRO 3410/Wat/3/50/8; 3/8/21–2; 3/64/37/3/109/44.

[33] *Mining Commissioner's Report*, Parliamentary Papers 1859, sess 2, Vol. 12, pp. 506–07. Standard designs of house are illustrated by Seeley, 'Mining villages,' pp. 286–96.

[34] Privy Council, *Report ... into the State of Popular Education*, Vol. 2, pp. 312–13; *Durham Chronicle*, 6 Jan. 1882.

1873 that on recent visits to his company's colliery houses he had found decided improvements. Some of the men were spending their money on books, pets, canaries, natural history collections of insects, etc. Most of the houses that his firm's workers lived in belonged to the company. It had built 525 houses between 1866 and the end of 1872, and had 200 more building. Pease was sure that the only way to get workers was to provide houses, and the men's expectations were, rightly, higher than they used to be. 'If you offer them an old-fashioned two-roomed colliery house, they shrug their shoulders before they will take your work; but if you offer them a four-roomed house with the back premises made comfortable and tidy, you engage your men much more easily; I mean a house with two rooms upstairs and two down.' The old houses, many of them with only two rooms, in the older mining districts, he would describe as 'perfectly unfit to live in,' if he had not seen worse at home and abroad. Two-roomed houses were built for £48–£60 each; four- and five-roomed houses cost between £108 and £120 to build. Joseph Pease and Partners generally provided gardens and pig-sties with their houses. Better housing encouraged men to stay: they became more settled; and 'even if you have no better motive than to keep your colliery going, it is worth doing.'[36] The Peases' experience was borne out by that of William Armstrong, the mining engineer, who in 1872 advised Bolckow Vaughan to build more cottages near their Auckland pits. Good cottages, he said, were now the chief means of ensuring large production. Every colliery proprietor was building, and 'vying with his neighbours in the scale of comfort they offer to entice and keep men.' It was no use to hope for regular workers or large production unless the men were well housed in a position near their work.[37]

Joseph Pease and Partners colliery houses generally enjoyed a good reputation for sound construction, spaciousness, and the provision of gardens. Instead of the earlier rows of houses, either built back to back or separated only by narrow lanes containing the privies and ash pits, the company experimented, at Roddymoor, Grahamsley, Waterhouses and Esh Winning, with houses built round a square. Waterhouses was described in the *Colliery Guardian* as a model village. During the 1870s many of the older houses were improved, the roof level of back bedrooms raised, and back yards enclosed with individual privies. By the 1880s most of the villages had a piped water supply.[38] A return of colliery-owned houses in 1874 indicates that whilst

[35]   John Holland, *The History and Description of Fossil Fuel, the Collieries and Coal Trade of Great Britain*, London 1835, p. 392; Leifchild, *Our Coal and Our Coal Pits*, pp. 208–09.

[36]   *Select Committee on Coal*, Parliamentary Papers 1873, Vol. 10, paras. 4308–9, 4329–31, 4364, 4400–06, 4416–20, 4460–2, 4470–2.

[37]   W. Armstrong to Bolckow Vaughan, 19 Oct. 1872, Northumberland Record Office, Armstrong Collection, NRO 725/B 8/117–18

[38]   *Newcastle Weekly Chronicle*, 'Our Colliery Villages' series, 15 Mar., 31 May, 28

Joseph Pease and Partners did not own any of the one-roomed cottages that still featured in villages belonging to the Earl of Durham, the Marquis of Londonderry and the Hetton Coal Company, the number of two-roomed houses that they owned was about the average even if the newer ones were bigger.[39]

From the public health point of view, most colliery villages in the North East in the middle of the nineteenth century left much to be desired, lacking as they did sewers, drainage, paved roads, and piped water. In these respects they were not worse than the working-class areas of large towns, and in some ways, being smaller, they suffered less disastrously from the lack of sanitation. Mortality rates were not higher than the average for urban working-class areas, but worse than those of agricultural villages. The chief obstacle to improvement was the structure of local government. Until 1872 sanitary administration was mostly the province of parish vestries, dependent on the willingness of ratepayers to spend money. Under the Public Health Act of 1872 areas not covered by incorporated boroughs or local boards of health were formed into rural sanitary authorities administered by the local poor law guardians. These authorities were given power to remove nuisances or require their removal, to repair wells and pumps, lay drains, and require house owners to drain their property. Still a great deal depended on property owners, who in colliery villages were often, although not always or wholly, the colliery owners. Some were conscientious, others were unwilling to spend more than the minimum; and small owners and ratepayers were often poor.[40] In some areas fresh water supply remained a problem until the end of the century, even in newer settlements.

The township of Crook and Billy Row contained the Peases West collieries and coke ovens, but the village of Crook itself was not colliery-owned. The township was the subject of one of the enquiries conducted for the General Board of Health in the 1840s and 50s after outbreaks of cholera. 'Being a new district, of accidental and rapid growth,' said the report, 'there has been little or no provision made for the drainage, either of houses, or the surface of the public thoroughfares.' A local builder said that he knew of no provision of drains for carrying off the soil from privies, and there was no system for removing the ashes. For water the people had to use wells (all except one privately owned) or springs. The total supply was inadequate, especially in summer. Witnesses described sharing one privy between six houses, sharing a pump between twenty families, lack of ash pits,

Jun., 12 Jul. 1873; Norman Emery, *The Deerness Valley. The History of a Settlement in a Durham Valley*, Durham 1988, p. 161; Emery, 'Pease and Partners,' p. 50.

39 Durham Coal Owners Association return, 1874, DCRO, National Coal Board Collection, NCB 1/Co/86/55.

40 Seeley, 'Mining Villages,' pp. 281–6; Church, *British Coal Industry*, Vol. 3, pp. 608–11; Benson, *British Coalminers*, pp. 95–103.

and having to repay borrowed water. There was opposition to the formation of a local board of health for Crook because it would cause expense; but the colliery owners, Joseph Pease and Partners and Bolckow Vaughan, supported it. In neighbouring Brandon Straker and Love opposed the creation of a board of health on the ground that it would put up the rates.[41]

Nearly twenty years later a reporter for the *Newcastle Chronicle* found that all the houses in Crook itself had privies, and most had some kind of drainage. Of the other villages in the township, North Roddymoor had, in addition to older rows, thirty newly-built four-roomed houses with water laid on to a tap in the yard; but the water, from a reservoir at Waskerley, was peat-stained and so far the inhabitants preferred to go on using a stream. The same was true at Stanley Crook, the entire settlement of which was built between 1860 and 1873 by Joseph Pease and Partners. All the houses there had gardens and privies, but some were already suffering from subsidence. At Sunnybrow, a Straker and Love village, the water supply was deficient and the privies inadequate, but there were some good houses. Billy Row, the oldest village in the township, did not have drainage in 1873 but got sewers and a water supply by 1880. Willington, another Straker and Love village, was one of the worst in the county: the houses were old, ill-ventilated and damp; privies and drains were inadequate; the drains ran in open ditches. In other parts of the county, all of the Earl of Durham's villages were said to have a water supply by 1858.[42]

By the nature of the coal industry, colliery owners had little direct personal contact with the men they employed except in the very smallest undertakings. The Peases did not live in the coalfield and coal was not their sole business enterprise. The kind of management and direct control found, for example, with the Cadburys and some other Quaker industrialists would have been most unlikely if not impossible for the Peases. Visits to the collieries were not rare, but neither were they very frequent. It was local managers, such as Thomas Douglas at Peases West and J. C. Crofton in the Deerness valley who attended concerts and patronised flower shows.[43] In trying to assess what difference their membership of the Society of Friends made to the Peases' record as colliery owners, one should compare them not only with other Quaker industrialists but also with other colliery owners. It does seem clear that the family took a more active and personal interest in

[41]   General Board of Health, *Report to the General Board of Health on a Preliminary Inquiry into the Sewerage, Drainage, and Supply of Water, and the Sanitary Condition of the Inhabitants of the Township of Crook and Billy Row, in the County of Durham*, London 1854, *passim*; Seeley, 'Mining Villages,' p. 220.

[42]   *Newcastle Weekly Chronicle*, 22 Feb., 8 Mar., 28 Jun., 5 Jul. 1873; Seeley, 'Mining Villages,' pp. 168–9, 174–6, 194–5, 200–01, 226–9; *Mining Commissioner's Report*, Parliamentary Papers 1858, Vol. 32, pp. 9–10.

[43]   Moore, *Pit-men, Preachers and Politics*, pp. 84–6.

education than other colliery owners, that they gave greater and more personal support to religious provision, that the quality of their housing was somewhat above the average. Although not themselves all teetotallers, they supported the temperance movement for social reasons, employed temperance missionaries, refused for some years to allow new pubs to open in their villages, were said to have sacked habitual drunkards, and encouraged the British Workman non-alcoholic public houses.[44] In many ways the Peases' social record is better than that of other colliery owners, and there is no reason not to attribute this to their Quakerism. They were also, on the whole, progressive in their attitude to industrial relations.

Before the 1870s many colliery owners were hostile to trade unions, refusing to allow their workers to unionise. As late as 1865 the Durham Coal Owners Association destroyed the union with the greatest potential membership; but by 1875 the county had 35,000 members of the Miners National Association, an organisation widely regarded as moderate, promoting accommodation with the owners and arbitration of disputes. The first systematic collective machinery appeared in Durham in 1872 with the formation of a joint committee of owners and union officials. Joseph Whitwell Pease told the Select Committee on Coal in 1873 that his company had recently joined the coal owners association, which he did not much like, because the joint conciliation committee seemed to be succeeding in improving industrial relations.[45] Joseph Whitwell Pease's attitude to trade unions was more favourable than that of some of his fellow colliery owners (and of some other Quaker industrialists); but he was clear that wage bargaining was not a proper role for them, and his view of a community of interest between employers and employees was paternalist. Opening a school at Esh in November 1871, after expatiating on the importance of education and offering the use of reading rooms for meetings, he said that he regarded trade unions as useful in so far as they could help the workers find the best market for their labour; but they should not try to meddle with prices, which were best left to the laws of supply and demand. He believed the master was under an obligation to pay the best price for labour according to the supply, if only in his own interest: 'It was a great advantage to employers when they had educated, steady, settled workpeople. It was to the comfort of the latter and the prosperity of the former. There was nothing so bad as when a master

44   Moore, *Pit-men, Preachers and Politics*, p. 83; Jeans, *Jubilee Memorial of the Railway System*, pp. 243–5.
45   *Report from the Select Committee on Coal*, Parliamentary Papers 1873, Vol. 10, paras. 4365–72. For the early history of trade unionism in the North East coalfield see Robert Fynes, *The History of the Northumberland and Durham Miners*, Sunderland 1873; G. H. Metcalf, *A History of the Durham Miners Association 1869–1915*, Durham 1947; Welbourne, *Miners' Unions;* John Wilson, *History of the Durham Miners' Association 1870–1904*, Durham 1907.

neglects his duty towards those whom he employs, and afterwards sees there is a feeling of discontent among his workmen, which he feels he ought to have prevented years before.'[46] At another school opening, at Stanley Crook in 1875, Joseph Whitwell Pease said that he had never admitted the existence of opposing interests between the employers and the employed, at any rate in the south Durham coalfield. Times had recently been difficult for both, with falling profits and falling wages. The company had thrown open their rooms to the unions wherever possible, believing and hoping that while the men were looking out for themselves they would also look at the employers' position, and the latter would try, while working for themselves, to look at the position of the men, so that employer and employed might 'go hand in hand not only for the benefit of each other, but for the benefit of the community at large'.[47]

In another speech in 1876 Joseph Whitwell Pease referred to the great rise in miners' wages in 1870 and 1871, and their subsequent fall to within 8 or 9% of the starting figure, all of which had taken place without anything that could be called a strike. He regarded this as a decided step in the progress of feelings between capital and labour. Arbitration had often been difficult, but in the end hardly anyone left without saying that their case had been quietly and well put. He was conscious of a feeling of great responsibility to do what was right and reasonable by the people whom the firm employed. Reports of this speech drew a rebuke from John Wilson, the Durham miners' leader, who thought the union was being praised for assisting in wage reduction instead of, as it had done, preventing still deeper cuts. Pease replied pacifically that he was sure he had not said what Wilson understood: he had simply expressed pleasure that recent reductions had been accomplished without strikes, and had commended arbitration.[48]

Joseph Whitwell Pease continued to speak out in favour of arbitration in the coal industry, finding himself in a minority in the Durham Coal Owners Association on the question in the strikes of 1879 and 1892.[49] But he also continued to oppose efforts to prevent companies requiring their employees to contract out of the Employers' Liability Act of 1880. In 1883 Thomas Burt, the first miner M.P., was promoting a bill to this effect. Sir Joseph argued in the House of Commons that workers should be allowed to judge for themselves whether the mutual funds that existed in a number of trades were more advantageous. For this he was denounced in the columns of the *Durham Chronicle* by a miner who accused him of hypocrisy in calling himself a

[46] *Durham Chronicle*, 24 Nov. 1871.
[47] *Durham Chronicle*, 15 Jan. 1875.
[48] *Durham Chronicle*, 10 Nov., 24 Nov., 1 Dec. 1876; *South Durham and Cleveland Mercury*, 11 Nov. 1876.
[49] *Durham Chronicle*, 2 May 1879, 2 Jun. 1897; Moore, *Pit-men, Preachers and Politics*, p. 87.

Liberal but putting his interests as an employer above the representation of the views of his constituents. Another miner then defended Pease's record of generosity in providing for the welfare of workers and the relief of widows and the injured. A third wrote that he had nothing against Pease personally but the firm's collieries were not paradise and its wages were no better than others'.[50] This exchange may stand as a fairly realistic reflection of the family's standing as colliery owners in local eyes. They were remembered as late as the 1960s by an elderly Methodist preacher in the Deerness valley as social and kind, interested in the affairs of the village, which felt it an honour to receive a visit.[51] On the whole the reputation may be said to have been earned.

[50]   *Durham Chronicle*, 15, 22, 29 Jun. 1883; *Parliamentary Debates*, 4th series, Vol. 280, cols. 506–10.

[51]   Moore, *Pit-men, Preachers and Politics*, p. 151.

CHAPTER FOUR
Local Politics

At the beginning of the nineteenth century Darlington, unlike its neighbour Stockton, did not have a corporation. It had been a seigneurial borough of the Bishop of Durham, and its affairs were still presided over by the bishop's chief bailiff, who filled the role occupied in a corporate borough by the mayor and whose duties by now were largely confined to calling public meetings. At this stage the absence of a corporation may have worked to Darlington's advantage, for until the Municipal Corporations Act of 1835 gave Dissenters their opportunity, no Quaker could have been a member.

Quaker influence in Darlington for much of the century was unusual, possibly unique. Other towns had as many and as important Quaker entrepreneurs and large Quaker communities; but in the large towns the entrepreneurs were outnumbered by non-Quakers. What made Darlington special was the Quaker predominance among local businessmen and Quaker numbers in proportion to the population of the town. The history of the community goes back at least to 1685, when two Quaker families were recorded. In 1776 Quaker numbers were estimated at 160.[1] On census day in 1851, 187 attended the morning meeting for worship and 167 in the afternoon. In 1864 Darlington Meeting had 277 members, with 116 'attenders.' By 1874 membership was 334, with 142 attenders; in the late 1870s and early 80s membership was over 400, with up to 250 attenders.[2] By way of comparison, in Bristol, which had a number of important Quaker entrepreneurs such as the Frys, attendance at meeting in 1851 was more than twice as large as in Darlington, but the population was more than eleven times the size. York, an important Quaker centre in the north of England, had a population in 1851 three times the size of Darlington, but attendance at meeting was only 50% higher. In the second half of the century York remained the larger of the two towns: Quaker membership figures were similar.[3] Kendal was much the same

---

[1] Robert Surtees, *History and Antiquities of the County Palatine of Durham*, Vol. 3, London 1823, p. 377; T. J. Nossiter, *Influence, Opinion and Political Idioms in Reformed England. Case Studies from the North East 1832-74*, Hassocks 1975, p. 129.

[2] DCRO, Darlington Monthly Meeting minute books, SF/Da/MM 1/11–16; *Diaries of Edward Pease*, p. 293.

[3] Allott, *Friends in York*, p. 78.

size as Darlington in the first half of the century, and had a strong Quaker community dating from the earliest days. Attendance at meeting in 1851 was comparable - 103 in the morning, 46 in the afternoon. But Kendal did not grow as Darlington did in the ensuing years, and the shoe-making firm that became its main industrial activity was not Quaker-owned.

Even after municipal reform in 1835 many Quakers were doubtful about accepting office. A committee of Newcastle Meeting recommended that no Friend could consistently accept the office of mayor, alderman, town clerk or councillor in any borough, or become a magistrate, on account of the declaration that would be required of him, that he would not do anything to injure or weaken the Church of England. Such an undertaking might be held to preclude any action about tithes or church rates; and as late as 1861 Friends were advised to weigh the import of the declaration very carefully before making it. Another difficulty lay in some of the possible duties of office, mayoral or magisterial, such as administering oaths, issuing warrants in connection with ecclesiastical demands (such as warrants for distraint of goods for refusal to pay church rates), or calling out the militia.[4] No Quaker was appointed a magistrate in County Durham until 1851, when Edmund Backhouse was made one in Sunderland. Quakers could, however, share with other substantial townsmen in the commissions which came into existence in the eighteenth and early nineteenth centuries as the first attempts to improve towns lacking drains, lighting or paving. A paving commission was set up for Darlington by a private act of Parliament in 1823, with power to have the streets paved and lit, to have nuisances removed, to set up a gas works, and to levy rates for the purposes. The commissioners were a self-perpetuating body, able to fill up their numbers without elections. Of the 131 named in the act, at least eighteen were Quakers, including seven Backhouses and seven Peases.[5] Members of the Pease family had been involved in philanthropic work in Darlington since the beginning of the century. For example Edward Pease was president, with Jonathan Backhouse, of the dispensary for the sick poor, opened in 1808; his mother, Mary Richardson, built four almshouses for the residence of poor widows.[6] Now the Peases became active in various forms of

[4] John William Steel, *A Historical Sketch of the Society of Friends in Newcastle and Gateshead*, Newcastle upon Tyne 1899, p. 80; Sansbury, *Beyond the Blew Stone*, pp. 167-8; Society of Friends, *Extracts from the Minutes and Epistles of the Yearly Meeting of the Religious Society of Friends, held in London from its First Institution to the Present Time, Relating to Christian Doctrine, Practice and Discipline*, 4th edn 1861, pp. 122-4. Quaker involvement in municipal government in York is discussed by Sheila Wright, *Friends in York. The Dynamics of Quaker Revival 1780-1860*, Keele 1995, pp. 85-97.

[5] 4 Geo. IV, c. iii, 18 Mar. 1823.

[6] W. Hylton Longstaffe, *The History and Antiquities of the Parish of Darlington in the Bishoprick*, Darlington and London 1854, pp. 266, 318; Surtees, *History and Antiquities of Durham*, Vol. 3, p. 377; M. A. Richardson, *The Local Historian's*

local administration as well as social bodies, and in promoting education and hospitals.

John Beaumont Pease served on the board of poor law guardians for thirty-two years and was chairman for fifteen.[7] Arthur Pease also served on the board of guardians for a number of years and was chairman for thirteen. The board of health, set up in 1850, was never without at least one Pease and usually more for the whole of its existence: Joseph was chairman for eight years. In addition to these bodies, members of the family were active in founding and running the mechanics' institute, the cottage hospital, the horticultural society, the school of art (i.e. design) and the teachers training college; and they supported local branches of the British and Foreign Bible Society, the British and Foreign School Society, the United Kingdom Alliance, and the Society for the Prevention of Cruelty to Animals. All these activities, along with their position as employers, formed a solid base for the Peases' influence in the town.

With the coming of the railway Darlington developed and the population grew – from 5720 in 1821 to 11,033 in 1847. New houses and villas were built, and in some of the main streets the footpaths were flagged.[8] But by 1848 dissatisfaction with the state of the town was widespread. The paving commissioners did not have power to compel occupiers to clean the streets; a newly created sanitary committee could not compel the provision of drains. The repair of highways was in the hands of three different surveyors appointed annually by the parish vestry. Nevertheless a meeting of ratepayers rejected a proposal for a new local act on the grounds of probable cost. Joseph Pease, who spoke in favour, said that he wanted the paving commission abolished and both sides of the question heard. 'He did not care who might tell him that the town was in a clean, healthy and respectable state; he thought quite otherwise. He thought the town was in a disgusting state in many respects and, for the sake of those who could not help themselves, he was anxious that something should be done to provide them with clean and healthy houses to live in. He would sign a petition for the Health of Towns bill whatever he might be taxed as a landlord, if he could make his tenants more comfortable. He wished the town to be in a very different situation as regards health and morals.'[9]

    Table Book of remarkable Occurrences ... Connected with the Counties of Newcastle-upon-Tyne, Northumberland and Durham, London 1841-6, Vol. 5, p. 196; Henry Spencer, *Men that are Gone from the Households of Darlington*, Darlington and London 1862, pp. 454-6.

[7] Memorial read on the evening of J. B. Pease's funeral, 18 Nov. 1873, DCRO, D/Pe 1/70.

[8] Francis Mewburn diary, 1825, DCRO, D/XD/55/1; Richardson, *Local Historian's Table Book*, Vol. 5, p. 196.

[9] *Darlington and Stockton Times*, 23 Nov., 30 Dec. 1848; Longstaffe, *History and*

The Public Health Act of 1848 had set up the General Board of Health, whose inspectors could enquire into the sanitary condition of towns. Only if the mortality rate was exceptionally high could an enquiry be imposed: other towns had to ask for one. In 1849 enough ratepayers were found in Darlington to petition for an enquiry; but there was resistance from a 'dirty party.' Some of this took an anti-Quaker form. Mewburn was called back from holiday to vindicate his position as chief bailiff against the 'grasping ambition and overweening vanity' of the sanitary committee now transformed into a transitional board of health, and present a loyal address to the Queen, who was to pass through Darlington. One of those who wrote to Mewburn told him; 'There will be *uproar* in the Town if the address is presented by a Quaker.' (It would probably have been John Pease.) No one, however, apparently objected to the Queen being given fruit and flowers from Henry Pease's garden, any more than they objected a few years later when the Dean of Durham, coming to preach in Darlington, stayed at Henry Pease's house. Only Mewburn observed, of this and another such occasion: 'Is it not singular that our Preachers should take up their abode with Friends. It shows that the Church of England has not many rich men in the town.'[10]

The Board of Health inspection was carried out in the autumn of 1849 by William Ranger. His report described the state of working-class housing in Darlington as 'truly deplorable,' with overcrowding, lack of ventilation, lack of drains, and dung heaps and privies close to doors and windows. There was a new waterworks and a contract to light the town with gas; but sewers were needed to remove the refuse from houses (at present the scavenger never came to the working-class areas), and they must not discharge into the river Skerne (which also received the waste from the Peases' Priestgate mill). Public wash houses were needed. A local board of health, elected by the ratepayers, should replace the paving commissioners.[11]

The first elections to the new board of health were held in September 1850. The eighteen members chosen included John, Joseph and Henry Pease. Thereafter until Darlington became a borough in 1867 the board never lacked members of the family – John, Joseph (both of whom served as chairman, between them for much of its history), Henry, John Beaumont, Joseph's sons Edward and Arthur, and John Beaumont's son Edwin Lucas – along with several Backhouses and other leading citizens. Each ratepayer with property

---

Antiquities of Darlington, p. 329.

[10] Mewburn, *Memoir of Fra: Mewburn*, pp. 31–2; *Durham Chronicle*, 28 Sep. 1849; Mewburn diary, 17 Mar. 1855, DCRO, D/XD/74/2.

[11] General Board of Health, *Report to the General Board of Health on a Preliminary Inquiry into the Sewerage, Drainage and Supply of Water, and the Sanitary Condition of the town of Darlington in the County of Durham*, London 1850; also a modern edition, ed. H. John Smith, *Public Health Act. Report to the General Board of Health on Darlington*, Durham 1967.

valued at under £50 had one vote; for every additional £50 value he or she – unlike the parliamentary franchise, women property-owners had a vote – got an additional vote, up to a maximum of six. An owner-occupier had a vote both as owner and as occupier. In 1862 there were 1235 electors, of whom 784 had one vote, 152 had two, forty had three, and six had four or more. The Peases between them, for their properties and as proxies for their business premises, were able to cast 118 votes out of a total of 2736.[12]

From the start the elections were warmly contested, and soon trouble arose over allegations of conflicts of interests. The first was about the abolition of town end tolls and the compensation to be paid to toll owners, of whom Henry Pease was one.[13] The next was over the purchase of the Darlington Gas and Water Company. This had been set up in 1849, with John Pease as chairman, Henry as one of the managing directors, and Joseph as a substantial shareholder; and it was suggested that Quaker support for a sanitary enquiry was connected with the prospect of profits from supplying water. The company's water came from the Tees and was at first not popular, being hard; but it was pure, and plentiful. The first task of the new board of health was to provide a complete system of drainage for the town. The board's surveyor, George Mason, recommended that it should buy or lease the works of the Gas and Water Company rather than set up another plant. Joseph and Henry Pease were convinced that the town needed a good water supply, but neither they nor the other directors and shareholders, including those on the board of health, wanted to sell a profitable undertaking. Eventually, under powers obtained under an Act of 1854, the company was bought out at a price that gave each shareholder double the amount he had invested only six years earlier.[14]

The Peases were not allowed to forget the charges of profiteering. One local newspaper commented that the ratepayers had not asked for the purchase, and 'the gentlemen who were acting for the ratepayers were precisely the same gentlemen who were bargaining for themselves ... Now these things look extremely awkward ... These proceedings have not only brought the Local Board of Health within suspicious limits, but they have positively attached a degree of cupidity to it. If gentlemen are so anxious to serve their own interest, do not let them do it at the expense of their constituents.'[15] As the local board obtained, by acts of Parliament in 1854 and 1861, additional powers to administer the town, so opposition to its domination by the Quaker elite grew. The opposition was led at first by Nicholas Bragg, a former Chartist, who was instrumental in forming a

12   Darlington Board of Health minute books 1859-76, DCRO, Da/a 1/1/1-2; poll book, 1862, D/DL/82/8; D/DL/22/8.
13   *Durham Chronicle*, 29 Aug., 5 Sep., 19 Sep. 1851.
14   Smith, *Public Health Act*, pp. 5-7.
15   *Northern Daily Express*, 24 Jun. 1856.

ratepayers' association and accused Joseph Pease of illegal trading in selling to the board products (pipes and coal) of the family companies. Joseph denied all knowledge of the transactions, and instructed his agents not to tender to the board; but Bragg returned to the charge a few years later.[16]

On two causes of Quaker concern the Peases were defeated in Darlington. At the end of 1859 an application for a license for a theatre was opposed by Henry Pease in a handbill distributed to the workers in the woollen mill. The *Darlington Telegraph* denounced him for attempting to confine the public in the 'gloomy bonds of an ascetic theology.' When the license application came before the magistrates in October 1860 Joseph Whitwell Pease, newly on the bench, opposed it but was outvoted. One of the other magistrates, a landowning Liberal Colonel G. J. Scurfield, commented that 'there is a sort of cloud pall hanging over the town, which seemed to swamp every sort of amusement'; and the police superintendent asserted that people leaving Band of Hope meetings were as noisy as those leaving the theatre.[17] Then came the formation of a corps of rifle volunteers. As pacifists the Peases were of course opposed to this: Henry had already objected to a similar proposal at Stanhope. A well-attended and noisy meeting at Darlington in July 1860 was commended by Colonel Scurfield for coming to a gathering 'not initiated by those of influence, wealth ... [and] of a religion opposing war who are of unbounded wealth and proud position.'[18]

Nevertheless the Peases and their relatives and Friends continued to dominate the elections to the board of health, and Bragg launched a campaign to have the town divided into wards. Such a change, which would reduce the effect of plural voting, was permitted under the Local Government Act but required the consent of the local board, and the Darlington board as presently constituted was certain to refuse. To get round the problem an amendment to the improvement bill currently before Parliament was needed. The amendment was sent to the Conservative M.P. for South Durham, James Farrer, but he was ill and Henry Pease, his opposite number, only got the letter as he was about to leave London at the end of the session. Henry did not present the amendment and was accused locally of deliberate sabotage. Both he and Joseph were denounced by the *Darlington Telegraph* as abettors of corruption: 'Too purse-proud to own themselves in the wrong, and practise what they preach – too selfish to allow others, if possible, even the freedom of thought.'[19]

The agitation then turned to demands for a municipal corporation and a parliamentary seat. John and Joseph Pease were against the corporation;

[16]   Smith, *Public Health Act*, pp. 12–13.

[17]   *Darlington Telegraph*, 19 Nov. 1859, 20 Oct. 1860.

[18]   *Darlington Telegraph*, 31 Dec. 1859, 21 Sep. 1861; *Durham Chronicle*, 20 Jul. 1860.

[19]   *Darlington Telegraph*, 27 Apr., 11 May, 24 Aug., 31 Aug., 21 Sep. 1861; *Durham Chronicle*, 13 Sep., 20 Sep.; Smith, *Public Health Act*, pp. 14–15.

Joseph Whitwell Pease, who became one of the M.P.s for South Durham in 1865, was in favour of parliamentary representation. The local board of health was divided on the corporation issue, and a ballot of ratepayers in April 1866 was inconclusive: 362 votes were cast in favour, 272 against; there were 388 abstentions, and 174 ballot papers were not returned. 'It is quite evident,' remarked the *Durham Chronicle*, 'that the majority of the members of the board are against a corporation, and from what was said at the meeting, there can be no doubt that they have regretted ever pledging themselves to support the wishes of the voting inhabitants ... In the end a corporation must come, and if all the inhabitants had been allowed to attend the meeting yesterday instead of only two or three "visitors," we are certain they would have left determined in their mind that the time has come when Darlington should adopt the Municipal Act of Incorporation.'[20] Joseph Pease, as chairman of the board of health, undertook to consult other towns on their experience, and reported the results to the ratepayers. He was himself totally against a corporation, arguing that the services now performed by the board and other competent authorities would cost more, that contested elections would bring in party strife, coercion and bribery, and that extension of the franchise would penalise property and deprive women ratepayers of their vote.[21]

In the autumn of 1866 the board of health was still unable to reach a decision. John and Joseph Pease retired but still, complained the *Durham Chronicle*, 'the place is ruled with an iron hand by those who, on the hustings, spout and harangue Liberal principles to the multitude, while at home they exercise a despotic sway by means of money, against which it is impossible to struggle. The ratepayers are not represented. The whole sway of the place is exercised by a clique, who have ordered election after election in such a manner that it would be a much more honest thing at the Board of Health if a resolution were passed that such and such nominees and dummies and sycophants sit without the farce of a pseudo-election at all ... Mr Pease would have retired from the world with much better grace and with a reputation much more untarnished, and with a comfort of his own existence infinitely greater, had he never dabbled in local politics.'[22] A move was now made to get the Chief Bailiff Francis Mewburn to call a meeting of ratepayers. 'The great grievance,' wrote the *Durham Chronicle*, 'is that of the power a few parties of enormous wealth and influence in the town possess in having a plurality of votes, by which they can, and do pack the board with their own nominees to the exclusion of those for whom more voters may give in their adhesion, though their aggregate number is represented by a minority of votes ... An

[20]   *Durham Chronicle*, 13 Apr, 1866; Smith, *Public Health Act*, pp. 16–17.
[21]   Joseph Pease handbill, 'Ought Darlington to have a Municipal Corporation? To the Ratepayers of Darlington,' quoted by Kirby, *Men of Business*, pp. 65–6. I have not been able to trace this document in the Durham County Record Office.
[22]   *Durham Chronicle*, 5 Oct. 1866.

amount of trafficking by members of the local government has been pursued without check or shame, and certain parts of the town ... are left in a disgraceful condition, and in strong contrast to the expense lavished on the more favoured quarters of the place in which the magnets [*sic*] reside.[23] The meeting, held on 13 November, was the liveliest the town had seen for years. On its eve John Pease published a handbill stating his opposition to a corporation. After recounting the changes and the progress made in Darlington in his lifetime, the share he had had in furthering most of the improvements, and the wise and honest management of the various boards, he maintained that in local government property should carry weight. Popular election was no guarantee of good government; a mayor and corporation giving a breakfast or dinner, a mayoress giving a ball, would not mean well-conducted affairs. The proposed change 'would not add to the material progress, good feeling, or morality in the town, but probably decrease these, whilst it would promote intemperance and dissipation, and materially increase our expenditure and rates.'[24]

The petition for a corporation was signed by 2,480 persons, and the charter was granted in September 1867. No member of the Pease family was present at the celebratory banquet, but the 'corporation party' rejoiced too soon. The leader of the party was Henry King Spark, a self-proclaimed independent Liberal, born at Alston, the son of a lead miner. Spark came to Darlington in the 1840s from Barnard Castle, and worked for the *Darlington and Stockton Times*. In Darlington he made money as a coal merchant and acquired colliery interests near Durham; but he was not a good businessman, he got into financial difficulties, and had to borrow from the large colliery owner Joseph Love. In 1869 Love bought him out, at a loss. Spark then took on two more collieries and bought the *Darlington and Stockton Times* and *Mercury*, which he used to further his political career.

As a 'new man' Spark became a notable figure in Darlington, but the first municipal elections showed the strength of the Pease influence in the town, able to put up family members and others as candidates, and showed also the disparate nature of the alliance of disaffected liberals, conservatives, and publicans who gathered round Spark. The town was divided into six wards, to be represented by three councillors each. Spark stood in the working-class east ward, and got in by a majority of only two votes, whilst Henry Pease (accused of using undue influence among the railway workers) came top of the poll. Altogether five Peases were elected, and Joseph and John Beaumont Pease were chosen as aldermen. Joseph was elected mayor, but declined on health grounds and was replaced by Henry. The latter had not relished the prospect of the 'interference, distraction, and probable (almost inevitable) association

<hr>

23 *Durham Chronicle*, 9 Nov. 1866.
24 John Pease handbill, 'To the Ratepayers of Darlington,' 10 Nov. 1866, DCRO, U 418f, 34471.

with uncongenial spirits' which the mayoralty would entail; but on the other hand he reflected: 'Has providence placed me in a position in which by being as it were the temporary rallying point of the respectable and intelligent of our Town the government under a corporation might at least have a fair start?'[25] Spark and his supporters put the best possible face on the results, claiming that the 'old bonds of influence and interest' had been loosened: the corporation party 'have given the deathblow to the old party government, and they have set their seal upon the freedom of the town.' But the hostile *Darlington and Stockton Telegraph* rejoiced that 'those represented by the party opposed to Mr Spark are not the embodiment of "an old and exclusive power whose roots were laid in corruption," they are the men who, without any seeking of their own, the burgesses had confidence in, whom they sought out by a requisition and triumphantly elected.'[26]

In the seventeen years of its existence the Darlington board of health not only bought the gas and waterworks but acquired the town hall (Joseph Pease gave a clock) and slaughterhouse, obtained power to make bye-laws, regulate the market and enlarge the market place, and extend the geographical bounds of its authority. By 1867 it was employing a medical officer, a surveyor, a rate collector, two inspectors of nuisances, a market keeper, and secretary, clerk and treasurer, at a total annual salary bill of £1,077 18s. Eighteen miles of sewers had been laid and the sewage outfall diverted; and water was laid on to all public streets. Generally speaking, living conditions for the poor improved.[27] The Peases and their friends were never charged with extravagance with the ratepayers' money: charges of corruption amounted at most to profiteering over water supply and securing posts for their protégés. The real ground of the opposition to them was that they monopolised membership of the local board through their own plural votes, their leadership of the Quaker community, and their position as large employers in the town, so that Darlington was in the hands of a small group of wealthy businessmen. The influence of these men was not immediately weakened by municipal reform: change came rather later, with growing population (from 11,582 in 1851 to 27,729 in 1871 and 35,104 in 1881) and a growing working-class and trade union vote. Spark meanwhile transferred his ambitions to the parliamentary front, and his career after 1867 is discussed in the next chapter.

The Pease influence in Darlington, south Durham and north Yorkshire was at its height in the 1870s. The family were widely praised for public spirit, sometimes in lyrical terms. The *Northern Echo*, for example, a Liberal paper

25 Henry Pease to John Pease, 1 Oct. 1867, DCRO, D/Ho/C 52/263; Henry Fell Pease diary, 12, 19 Dec., D/Pe 5/22.
26 *Darlington and Stockton Times*, 7 Dec. 1867; *Darlington Mercury*, 4 Dec.; *Darlington and Stockton Telegraph*, 23 Nov., 30 Nov., 7 Dec.
27 Smith, *Public Health Act*, pp. 12, 18.

which Pease money had helped to set up, described their influence as 'not merely territorial or industrial. It is one of the healthiest of all influences – that exerted by public-spirited citizens, who are ever to be found in the forefront of the hottest battles ... They have been, and still are, the leaders of the [South Durham parliamentary] Division, in nearly every good work, political, social, moral or industrial ... Some of them are a curious combination of the millionaire and the missionary, with the means of the former and the zeal of the latter ... It is almost impossible to call to mind any class equally extensive which possesses such a singularly high moral standard as the average attained by its members ... They are remarkably free from pride of birth, the pride of power, the pride of purse. Many of them recognize and habitually act upon the principle that they are but stewards of the wealth and influence which they possess, and they administer their trust with stern conscientiousness and scrupulous exactitude.'[28]

A couple of years later the *Durham Chronicle*, which had been very critical of the Peases over the corporation issue, praised them as employers, writing: 'We apprehend that there are few commercial firms in this or any other county who enjoy so wide and well-deserved reputation for the faithfulness with which they discharge their duty to the masses of men and youths whom they employ at their different undertakings as the great House of South Durham. Their exertions and sacrifices on behalf of education have placed them in the front rank of those who make it a matter of conscientious duty to promote the intellectual well-being of the people who toil for them by hard manual labour; and it is not too much to say, that if all who profit by the industry of large bodies of workmen were to set up for themselves the same high standard of duty, and to give practical effect to what they admit to be their obligations in such matters,' the effect in the whole district would be enormous.[29] At the same time a local Quaker apologist, John William Steel, celebrated the work and influence of the Friends in Darlington, which he called the English Philadelphia. Whilst accounting for less than 10% of the population, Quakers 'still largely constitute the power and the governing bodies of the town.' Seven of the nine mayors chosen since the town became a borough had been Quakers; one third of the aldermen and of the school board were Friends. 'Largely gifted with wealth, these Quakers are lavish in its use for the town – their purses exuding schools, cemeteries, chapels, furnishing the bulk of splendid training colleges.'[30] Four of the seven mayors referred to were Peases – Henry (twice), Arthur, Henry Fell and Edwin Lucas, along with Edward Kipling, Alfred Kitching and Charles Ianson. Later John Pease's

28 Northern Echo, *The Durham Thirteen*, pp. 142–3.
29 *Durham Chronicle*, 10 Nov. 1876.
30 John William Steel, 'The English Philadelphia,' in *'Friendly Sketches.' Essays Illustrative of Quakerism*, London and Darlington 1876, pp. 92–6.

two sons-in-law, Theodore Fry and Jonathan Backhouse Hodgkin were mayor in, respectively, 1877–8 and 1884–5. Thereafter the involvement in local politics diminished, but Jack Pease was mayor in 1889–90, and William Edwin, Edwin Lucas Pease's son, in 1902–3.

CHAPTER FIVE
National Politics

The story of the Pease family in parliamentary politics illustrates and to some extent epitomises the evolution both of British politics between 1832 and 1914 and of the standing and attitudes of a Dissenting business clan. In this chapter the process will be examined that led from the first parliamentary candidacy in 1832 – a candidacy that would have been virtually unthinkable in a county seat before that date – to the figure of four or five Peases and close relatives in Parliament after 1885. It is not a story of high politics: before the turn of the century the Westminster game was of secondary importance to these men; it was much more a matter of personal standing and representing principles and local interests. In attempting to estimate the Peases' local political standing and influence it has to be borne in mind that the North East throughout the period was a Liberal stronghold. Between 1832 and 1867 Liberals at no time held fewer than nine out of the thirteen seats in County Durham and Tyneside; after the Second Reform Act they lost only two out of sixteen seats in 1868, one in 1874, and none in 1880. By their background and occupation the Peases were bound to be Liberals. They therefore made their political way not against the tide but with it; but at a time when party allegiances were often fluid and party organisation non-existent, their progress illustrates the changes that took place in the composition of the political elite as well as of the electorate, as the landed class slowly gave way to industrialists, and the professional middle classes to some extent to commerce.[1]

The 1832 Reform Act added about 50% to the electorate in England and Wales; 143 very small boroughs were disfranchised or lost one member, and 41 new parliamentary boroughs were created. Nine counties had their representation increased. In Durham this meant new seats for Sunderland, Gateshead, and South Shields, and the county was divided into two with two seats each. The total electorate for the whole area was just under 10,000.

Even before the Parliament which had passed the Reform Act was dissolved, a group of influential men decided to put forward Joseph Pease as a candidate for South Durham in the forthcoming election. The names of the group are not recorded, but it is safe to assume that Francis Mewburn, the solicitor for the Stockton and Darlington Railway, was a leading member. In Mewburn's words, 'The object which Mr P's friends had in view was to

[1]   Nossiter, *Influence, Opinion and Political Idioms*, pp. 21–2.

throw out Mr [Robert Duncombe] Shafto in consequence of his want of application to business and because he was ... supported by the Aristos who could not allow of a commercial man being proposed to represent the division. It was urged that this division contained many great and important commercial establishments which required the fostering care of an intelligent representative.'[2] Joseph Pease at first hesitated to accept the proposition; and his family were mostly opposed, on religious grounds. Writing to his brother John, Joseph reported that their father 'expressed his decided opinion that unless I was wholly regardless of all parental counsel, the advice of all my best friends, the domestic happiness of my family, my duties as a husband and a parent, and a member of the Society of Friends, I could not for a moment entertain the idea of yielding under any contingency to become a representative of my countrymen in Parliament ... He seemed astonished that there could exist a doubt in my mind as to the wisest and safest course.'[3] Eventually Edward and the rest of the family abandoned their opposition, whilst remaining unenthusiastic, and when a deputation inviting Joseph to stand called at his summer holiday quarters at Seaton Carew on 14 August 1832 he asked, largely as a matter of form, for a few days to prepare his reply and then accepted, stressing his independence and the sacrifices he would be making. 'If,' he said, 'I am elected freely and spontaneously, by a generous and free people – if you can forego all ancient prejudices – if you can approve my stedfast [sic] adherence to my religious faith and practice – if you will support me in my purpose to maintain a manly independence in and out of Parliament – an independence becoming your Representatives, and indispensable to their dignity – an independence which admits not of coarse and vulgar ribaldry, recrimination or scurrility – no hiring of Agents to prejudice, terrify or seduce unwary voters – no semblance of overpersuading, or mercenary inducement – if you send me, bearing on my front this motto:– "The free and unbought representative of a free and unsold people," then I cannot conscientiously refuse to tender myself to the House of Commons as the man of your choice, there to prove myself uncorrupted and incorruptible ... I am bold to remind you, that the high distinction you desire to confer upon me has been unsought by me – that no career of ambition is before me – the law itself withholds from me all temptation of office or emolument through a course of political subserviency – and that, in resigning myself to your service, the sacrifices I make of domestic comfort and happiness, of time, of expence [sic], and convenience, is not light. Contrast, yourselves, the charms of private life with the disquietude and turmoil of public affairs. I repeat that whilst I do not solicit your votes as a favour, I will gratefully receive them with honest pride as a sacred trust.'[4] Having accepted, Joseph wrote to his mother-in-law

[2]   Mewburn, *Larchfield Diary*, pp. 29–32, DCRO, D/XD/55, pp. 165–9.
[3]   *Diaries of Edward Pease*, p. 65.
[4]   *Durham Chronicle*, 24 Aug. 1832; *The Electors' Scrap Book*, Durham 1832; DCRO,

Jane Gurney, whose disapproval he expected: 'I have answered it – That I will not canvass, I will not ask one man for his vote, I will go to no expense, I will both in and out of Parliament unflinchingly support my practice and my profession as a member of the Society of Friends; if elected under these circumstances I will endeavour to serve them faithfully. I have counted the cost I trust – sacrifices in business, in ease, in quiet, in domestic comfort, but in my conclusion, after intense bitterness, I have been peaceful and comfortable. How much is my heart torn in thinking that distress and dismay may cover thy mind in reading these lines; if I am right, mayst thou be permitted to see it and feel it. If I am wrong, mayst thou be enabled to put up thy prayers with mine, for help in danger and in difficulty.'[5]

Misgivings such as those of Mrs Gurney and Edward Pease were not unusual. Joseph John Gurney, banker, anti-slave trade campaigner, and first cousin of Joseph Pease's wife, spent much of the winter of 1832–3 wrestling with the problem of whether standing for parliament and bearing there testimony to the cause of Christianity was compatible with his calling as a Quaker minister. He eventually decided against, and never regretted the decision.[6] Nine years later the mother-in-law of John Bright, anti-Corn law campaigner and the only Quaker to make a real name in politics in the nineteenth century, remonstrated with him for going into Parliament. He replied that he was often concerned lest so much public occupation should harm his better feelings and higher objects, but he did not think that public action in the ant-Corn Law cause was more dangerous than quieter participation. The cause itself was good, and he would feel guilty if he left the struggle entirely to others.[7] The Yearly Meeting, however, whilst acknowledging the duty of Friends to promote social betterment, went on for some years uttering warnings against party politics and 'meddling with political affairs.'[8]

Joseph Pease made up his mind, and despite his perhaps rather extravagant protestations of independence and reluctance, he did in fact campaign in all the principal towns and villages of this still essentially rural constituency with just under 4400 electors: only Bishop Auckland, Barnard Castle, Darlington, Middleton in Teesdale, Staindrop, Stanhope, Stockton and

---

Strathmore Papers, D/St/C 1/16/60(1).

[5] *Diaries of Edward Pease*, pp. 65–6. John Pease's attitude was expressed in a letter he drafted in reply to an invitation to dine with Joseph's committee after the election: the family had found the whole business trying, but were sensible of the honour done to Joseph and the marks of attention paid to them. John's speech at the dinner was probably much in this vein: DCRO, D/Ho/C 48/77.

[6] Joseph John Gurney, *The Memoirs of Joseph John Gurney*, ed. Joseph Bevan Braithwaite, Norwich 1854, Vol. 1, pp. 481–4; Swift, *Joseph John Gurney*, pp. 100–04.

[7] G. M. Trevelyan, *The Life of John Bright*, London 1913, pp. 102–03.

[8] Society of Friends, *Epistles from the Yearly Meeting*, Vol. 2, pp. 332, 334 (1846, 1848).

Wolsingham had more than 100 voters each.[9] He had to counter the charge of being opposed to the farming interest, and did so in a speech at Darlington market and in letters to the Tory *Durham County Advertiser*, saying that whilst he was in favour of cheap food he wanted to protect agriculture and represent everyone. At the same time Mewburn stressed the importance of the growing commercial interest of the Darlington area: 'They all knew how important this district had become – and that as the Port of the Tees was fast rivalling those of the Tyne and the Wear, it was important that they should have a man who could adequately represent the vast interests connected with it, as well as be attached to the Agricultural interest.'[10]

The Liberal *Durham Chronicle* favoured Joseph Pease from the start. 'It must be peculiarly satisfying to every friend of freedom,' it wrote, 'to see ... "the barriers of ancient prejudices" so signally broken down as they have been in the case of Mr Pease, who, Quaker though he be and offensive as he, on that count, may be to the imagination of the orthodox, has made such rapid progress, in the affections and good opinion of the Electors, as truly deserves to be called miraculous, even in this age of wonders. It is a glorious triumph of reason and liberality over ignorance and bigotry, which must lead to the happiest results.'[11] Mewburn believed that the gentry's assertion of a claim to the right to return both members for the division 'roused the energies of the people. In every large town in the division Mr Pease soon became the popular candidate ... and altho some farmers were to the last opposed to him yet by far the greatest proportion soon became convinced that he was their best friend.'[12]

Most of the large landowners in South Durham, according to Mewburn, were opposed to Joseph Pease, warning their tenants not to vote for him. The Marquis of Cleveland (shortly to be made a duke), who as Earl of Darlington had opposed the Stockton and Darlington Railway and the Darlington Quakers, was the greatest of the landlords and a Whig. Joseph Pease, accompanied by his father, called at Raby and was received courteously. The marquis dwelt on the sacrifices (of some pocket boroughs) he had made in helping to bring about the Reform Act. He took it quite for granted that his tenants should defer to his judgment, which was that John Bowes and Robert Duncombe Shafto, both neighbouring landowners, were the candidates best fitted to represent the agricultural part of the county. The marquis was, however, rather alarmed at being told that his land agent and the vicar of Staindrop had been threatening men with his displeasure if they did not vote

9   List of townships in South Durham and number of electors, DCRO, Strathmore Papers, D/St/C 1/16/45.
10   *Durham Chronicle*, 24 Aug. 1832; *Durham County Advertiser*, 7 and 24 Aug.
11   *Durham Chronicle*, 24 Aug. 1832.
12   Mewburn diary, DCRO, D/XD/55, pp. 165–9; Mewburn, *Larchfield Diary*, pp. 29–32.

for Bowes and Shafto; but even when he admitted that the area now had a large mining influence as well, his visitors thought he found it difficult to come to terms with the new idea. [13]

The election took place in November. In two-member constituencies electors had two votes each. If they 'plumped' for only one candidate they only exercised one vote, but denied the second to any other candidate. Joseph Pease came top of the poll with 2273 votes, Bowes second with 2218, and Shafto third with 1871. As could have been expected, Pease did best in the Darlington and Stockton polling districts, and benefited from votes split with Bowes in Barnard Castle and Stanhope districts. In the Bishop Auckland district more votes were split between Pease and Shafto than between the two landowners. This district included Shafto's father's estate of Whitworth; it also included the Peases' new collieries, and the palace of the Bishop of Durham. Bishop William Van Mildert was a Tory: later the episcopal influence shifted according to the views of the bishop of the day. [14] Barnard Castle included Bowes's estate at Streatlam as well as Raby. Upper Teesdale was exclusively Cleveland territory, and Pease's hope of getting 100 votes there were disappointed. Another area where Pease's support was comparatively weak was Sedgefield, rural and dominated by Lord Londonderry's estate at Wynyard. [15] Joseph Pease's success was hailed by a Tyneside bard as a defeat for 'Dean and Chapterism.' [16] In fact the cathedral chapter does not seem to have exercised much political influence in South Durham in 1832 or later, despite its position as the owner of coal royalties. Ecclesiastical leases were a bone of political contention in North Durham; and the chapter was naturally powerful in the city of Durham itself although never unanimous nor unquestioningly deferential to Lord Londonderry. [17]

When the new parliament met in January 1833 Mewburn accompanied Joseph Pease to London to take his seat. He was the first Quaker to be elected, and although Quakers had been able to affirm in law courts since 1721, there was no precedent for affirmation in place of the oath of allegiance required of M.P.s. Mewburn had studied the law carefully, felt that his reputation as a lawyer was at stake, and was shocked at the ignorance displayed by members, ministers, and even the Speaker. After much discussion a select committee was appointed to investigate the matter, and reported that Joseph was entitled to be admitted on his affirmation. He took his seat on 15 February 1833, and made his maiden speech on the subject of coastal light dues, a subject of interest to himself and his constituents in

13 Edward Pease to John Pease, 6 Sep. 1832, DCRO, D/Ho/C 52/180.
14 Nossiter, *Influence, Opinion and Political Idioms*, pp. 55–7. Shafto went on to represent North Durham from 1847 to 1868.
15 Analysis of poll books, Mewburn diary, DCRO, D/XD/55, pp. 165–9.
16 'Reform!!! The End of the Chapter,' North Shields, printed by W. Grey 1832.
17 Nossiter, *Influence, Opinion and Political Idioms*, pp. 122–3.

connection with Tees navigation.[18]

In the House of Commons Joseph Pease spoke fairly often, on subjects such as anti-slavery, church leases, the corn laws (on which he continued to hedge), railways, and coal. He claimed, soon after he took his seat, that he was made a target for attacks from all quarters; but he became known as a useful member, extremely punctilious in attendance and displaying intelligence and good judgment. He spoke too fast and his voice was not strong. In accordance with Quaker principles, he did not use honorific forms of address to anyone.[19] In the 1835 election Pease and Bowes were returned unopposed, Shafto having withdrawn and the Tories having found that they had no chance of success. Joseph's fellow directors on the Stockton and Darlington Railway gave him a number of free tickets to bring supporters to Darlington from Stockton and Shildon on nomination day; but they were outshone by Bowes's supporters, a band of 'hardy independent voters' from Weardale who had been well organised and cheered as agreed, and a body of yeomanry from Raby and Streatlam with a band and flags, who looked very ornamental when drawn up in front of the King's Head inn but had not been organised and never opened their mouths. While Joseph was addressing the electors the hustings collapsed, but sank slowly so that no one was injured: only a few ladies in the windows opposite fainted. After the proceedings Bowes gave his friends a cold collation at the King's Head; Joseph's friends gave him a dinner at the Sun Inn.[20]

Two years later the death of William IV caused another election. Once again Bowes and Pease were returned unopposed. Joseph had thought of retiring, but his partners and friends urged him to stand again and he bowed to their pressure. There was also an attempt to unseat him, mounted by the group round the Clarence Railway which was angered by his opposition to the Durham South West Railway bill. Threats were uttered about what would happen if Joseph put himself forward again, but in the event no other candidate appeared and the declaration passed off peacefully.[21]

In 1841, however, Joseph Pease resolved to retire from Parliament. His father had never really been reconciled to his membership, even while he admitted that it had been useful to local concerns; and Joseph himself had become frustrated at the lack of progress in reform in the last few years, and

18 Mewburn diary, Feb. 1833, DCRO, D/XD/55, pp. 226–7; Mewburn, *Larchfield Diary*, pp. 29–32..

19 *Parliamentary Debates*, 3rd ser., Vol. 18, col. 687; James Grant, *Random Recollections of the House of Commons, from the Year 1830 to the Close of 1835 ... by One of No Party*, London 1836, pp. 289–91.

20 Mewburn diary, Jan. 1835, DCRO, D/XD/55, pp. 226–7; Mewburn, *Larchfield Diary*, pp. 38–9; report for Bowes, Strathmore Papers, D/St/C 1/16/261; Tomlinson, *North Eastern Railway*, p. 418.

21 Mewburn diary, Aug. 1837, DCRO, D/XD/55, pp. 282–3; Mewburn, *Larchfield Diary*, p. 46.

by the party rancour inside and outside the House of Commons. What seems to have been the deciding factor was John Pease's virtual withdrawal from business in order to concentrate on religious work. In these circumstances Joseph evidently decided that he must give all his time to the family's increasingly complex business affairs.[22] In his farewell address to the electors of South Durham Joseph referred with pride to the reforms achieved since 1832 and his own record of service: they might, he said, find a more talented representative but would not easily find one who worked harder. The local Liberal press regretted Joseph's departure and was confident that he would be accompanied into private life by the respect and esteem not only of Liberals but even of 'respectable and influential' Tories.[23] Joseph's place was taken by Lord Harry Vane, youngest son of the Duke of Cleveland, a Whig like his father whereas the elder sons, who succeeded to the dukedom in turn between 1842 and 1864, were Tories. The 1841 election was contested. In addition to Bowes and Vane there was a Conservative candidate, James Farrer, half-brother of the Earl of Eldon. In the event Farrer came quite a long way third, with 1739 votes to Bowes's 2576 and Vane's 2512. Vane was careful to respect the convention by which tenants voted according to their landlord's wishes, and refrained from canvassing Wynyard territory. He also observed the convention that a candidate should not ask his own (or his family's) tenants to share their votes with another candidate even of the same party.[24] The election proceedings were marked throughout by disorder, especially when Bowes came to Darlington on 28 June. As in 1835 there was a fine cavalcade of electors from Weardale, but a group of Farrer supporters rendered Joseph Pease's and Bowes's speeches inaudible by 'hooting, roaring and bellowing.' The day ended with battles among the mob and between them and the police, and windows were broken.[25]

The next two elections, in 1847 and 1852, were uncontested, Bowes retiring and the representation of South Durham being shared between Vane and Farrer. Such sharing was common, and contests took place in fewer than half the constituencies in the 1840s and 50s, when party alignments in Parliament were often fluid and elections were expensive.[26] In South Durham Vane, after his father's death in 1842, was in the somewhat awkward position

---

22 *Diaries of Edward Pease*, p. 166 (10 Jun. 1840); Joseph Pease diary, 28 May, 4 Jun., 5 Jun. 1841, J. G. Pease Papers.

23 *Durham Chronicle*, 11 Jun., 18 Jun. 1841.

24 Nossiter, *Influence, Opinion and Political Idioms*, p. 48.

25 Joseph Pease diary, 28 Jun. 1841, J. G. Pease Papers; Richardson, *Local Historian's Table Book*, Vol. 5, pp. 273–5; Fordyce, *History and Antiquities of Durham*, Vol. 1, p. 456.

26 David Cresop Moore, *The Politics of Deference. A Study of the Mid-Nineteenth Century English Political System*, Hassocks 1976, pp. 282–5; F. W. S. Craig, *British Electoral Facts 1832–1987*, 5th edn, Aldershot 1989, p. 160.

of being the Liberal nominee of his Tory brother. In 1847 he hesitated about standing. Joseph Pease, who despite having retired from parliament retained his interest in politics, advised Vane to say nothing at all, and the election passed off quietly, to the disappointment of some electors who would have liked the opportunity of defeating Farrer.[27] Joseph nominated Vane again in 1852; but in 1857 Darlington interests were no longer willing to acquiesce in the Vane–Farrer arrangement, and Henry Pease was put up as a second Liberal candidate. The prospect of a contest, and the opportunity for the Liberals of South Durham to demonstrate that the representation of the division was not in the hands of one or two great families, pleased the *Durham Chronicle*. It hoped for the return of 'men of enlightened and progressive views,' and urged voters to split for Vane and Pease. Both held the broad principles of Liberalism and progress, as against the obstructionist views of Farrer. 'In Lord Harry Vane they have an old, a tried, and valued servant – one who has done them much good service and may continue to do so for many years. In Mr Pease they have a man of thorough honesty, of great commercial enterprise, of sound and broad principles, and of habits and experience acquired during a successful commercial life, which renders him peculiarly fitted to represent a constituency whose commercial importance is rapidly rising.'[28]

Vane himself did not want to appear in coalition with Henry Pease, and his brother tried to reconcile conflicting family and political loyalties by instructing his tenants to split their votes between Vane and Farrer. This was a mistake. Even in Barnard Castle district more votes were divided between the two Liberals than between Vane and Farrer: the duke had evidently overstepped the proper bounds of influence. Farrer did better than in his last contest in 1841, gaining 2091 votes; but he still came third. He did best for plumpers in Bishop Auckland, Sedgefield and Stockton districts, and in Hartlepool where Ralph Ward Jackson's feud with the Peases was at its height. Henry Pease came top of the poll with 2570 votes, Vane second with 2545. Some voters in Darlington did not like splitting between Pease and Vane but were persuaded by the Pease committee to do so.[29] Edward Pease, now a very old man, whilst glad of the proof that South Durham was not in the sole power of the duke, was characteristically worried about Henry's spiritual well-being. 'The decision as regards my precious son yields me no comfort,' he wrote in his diary. 'My fears and forebodings are in some degree those of

---

27   Joseph Pease diary, 4 Aug. 1847, J. G. Pease Papers; Nossiter, *Influence, Opinion and Political Idioms*, p. 52.

28   *Durham Chronicle*, 20 Mar., 3 Apr. 1857.

29   South Durham poll book, 1857; J. W. Pease diary, 31 Mar., 3 Apr. 1857; Joseph Pease diary, 22 Mar., 1 Apr., 3 Apr., 4 Apr., J. G. Pease Papers; Mewburn diary, 3 Apr., DCRO, D/XD/23/2., pp. 181–3; Mewburn, *Larchfield Diary*, p. 165; Nossiter, *Influence, Opinion and Political Idioms*, p. 53.

apprehension that it will not be for his soul's peace or that this dear Son may be exposed to temptation and discomforts.' And again, 'My mind does not derive comfort from dear Henry's election, but as an increase of virtuous right-minded men in the House of Commons is greatly to be desired, so I desire that merciful over-riding goodness may permit some enduring good to spring out of what my dear Son does consider to be his right and proper state.'[30]

The Duke of Cleveland learned the lesson, and when in 1859 another election was called Vane, having started to campaign, suddenly withdrew. He was given to understand that the Raby tenants would be instructed to plump for Farrer. Whether they would have done so cannot be known – there was some evidence of defiance at Stanhope; but the consequences to them of disobeying orders could have been serious, and Vane, offered the chance of a seat elsewhere, chose not to divide the family. The South Durham Liberals, who were sure of winning both seats, were angry; the Peases urged Vane to go on; the *Durham Chronicle* denounced Tory landowners. But it was too late to produce another Liberal candidate with a good chance, and so Henry Pease and Farrer were returned unopposed.[31]

Henry Pease represented South Durham in Parliament from 1857 to 1865. He was regular in his attendance, became known as a useful member, and spoke fairly often on such subjects of local interest as harbours of refuge on the north-east coast, the employment of children under 12 in mines, and railway regulation, and of personal interest such as closing of public houses on Sundays and enabling Jews to sit in Parliament. A few items of his constituency correspondence survive, unlike that of his brother and his nephew, which has unfortunately been destroyed. They show Henry exercising a modest degree of local patronage in nominating persons for sub-postmasterships.[32] But he did not like London and the late hours, and in 1865 was glad to hand over the seat to his nephew Joseph Whitwell Pease. Lord Harry Vane's succession as fourth Duke of Cleveland brought that family's influence back to the Liberals, but there was a good deal of confusion about the subsequent election. A second Liberal candidate was found in Captain Frederick Beaumont, a member of a family with large lead-mining interests in Weardale; but there was some resistance to him among more radical Liberals, he took his time in appearing in the constituency, and the Cleveland influence was not thrown behind him. On the Conservative side Farrer announced his retirement: this seemed to offer the Liberals the

30   *Diaries of Edward Pease*, pp. 343–4, 3 and 6 Apr. 1857.
31   *Durham Chronicle*, 15 Apr., 22 Apr., 29 Apr., 20 May. 3 Jun. 1859; J. W. Pease diary, 18–26 Apr., 3 May, J. G. Pease Papers; Nossiter, *Influence, Opinion and Political Idioms*, p. 53.
32   W. G. Hayter, Treasury, to H. Pease, 17, 26 Dec. 1857, 7 Jan. 1858, DCRO, D/DL/9/12–14.

prospect of an overwhelming victory; but then Henry Pease's decision to retire emboldened the Conservatives to put forward a new candidate, Colonel Charles Surtees, a popular member of a local landowning family. The result was that Surtees came second in the poll, with 3211 votes to Joseph Whitwell Pease's 3401. Beaumont was third with 2925 votes. The *Durham Chronicle* attributed the disaster to overconfidence on the part of the business and industrialist Liberals in face of Tory charges that South Durham would become a Quaker-dominated constituency.[33] There was rather more to it than that. The electorate had grown and was changing. Stockton, Darlington and Hartlepool had all grown so much in population that they could expect to be given seats in any new redistribution, but meanwhile their urban freeholders were county electors. Most observers assumed that they would vote Liberal. Mewburn, for example, thought that the increase in the number of freeholders would consign the landowners to 'insignificant influence' in the future, unless 'a large body at one of these towns' allied itself with a Conservative landowner. In 1865 that happened in Hartlepool, where Jackson still exerted great influence. In this district the Conservatives secured 9% more of the vote than in the constituency overall. Another factor, not considered by Mewburn, was the possibility of an urban Radical challenge to the Liberal notables but that threat was not yet serious.[34]

The Peases could now, in effect, ensure that one of their number could be returned to Parliament whenever they chose; and from 1857 they always chose at least one. It has been calculated that the Pease interest was worth at least 200 votes as early as 1832, and was probably as much as 1000 (out of an electorate of 7000) by 1865. The influence in the middle of the century was exercised largely by the network of business connections and of the Society of Friends, and in Darlington directly by the Peases as employers. Whilst some effort was put into registering electors, there was virtually no continuing party political organisation in South Durham before 1865, only *ad hoc* committees of local personages for the few weeks of campaigning before an election.

The Reform Acts of 1867 and 1868 created nine new borough constituencies, among them Darlington, Stockton, Hartlepool and Middlesbrough. The borough franchise was made uniform, but the county franchise was not affected. The total electorate for the area between the Tyne and the Tees nearly trebled, from a little over 20,000 in 1865 to something over 56,000

---

[33]   *Darlington and Stockton Times*, 27 Aug., 10 Sep., 17 Sep., 22 Oct., 29 Oct., 5 Nov., 12 Nov., 26 Nov. 1864, 27 May, 10 Jun., 17 Jun., 1 Jul., 15 Jul., 22 Jul. 1865; *Durham Chronicle*, 9 Sep., 16 Sep., 23 Sep., 30 Sep., 7 Oct., 28 Oct., 11 Nov. 1864, 19 May, 16 Jun., 23 Jun., 30 Jun., 7 Jul., 14 Jul., 21 Jul., 28 Jul. 1865; J. W. Pease diary, Jun.–Jul. 1865, J. G. Pease Papers; Nossiter, *Influence, Opinion and Political Idioms*, pp. 46, 53.

[34]   Mewburn, *Larchfield Diary*, p. 199; Nossiter, *Influence, Opinion and Political Idioms*, pp. 68–9.

in 1868. Most of the increase was in the boroughs, old and new; North Durham grew by about 40%, South Durham by about 22%. For the first general election after these changes it was thought that the enfranchisement of the new boroughs might weaken the Liberal position in South Durham, but the party had revived since the failure of 1865, and effort had been put into registration of voters.[35] At first a contest was not expected; but in the event Capt. Beaumont reappeared, taking the Peases by surprise, and Surtees was joined by the Hon. Gustavus Hamilton Russell, son of Lady Boyne who owned coal royalties round Brancepeth.[36] Pease and Beaumont came first and second, with 4321 and 4021 votes respectively, Surtees third with 3746, and Russell 3215 – he came top in Bishop Auckland district, which included the Boyne estates.

Events in Darlington were much more exciting. Here a 75-strong election committee, created by the town's Liberal Registration Society, chose as the official Liberal candidate Edmund Backhouse, senior partner in the family bank, a Quaker, and a cousin of the Peases. At one stage Henry Fell Pease, Henry's son, had considered putting himself forward, but in view of the bitterness shown in the recent borough elections, described in Chapter 4, he decided not to stand. Backhouse had been suggested as a candidate for South Durham in 1852, and had not been involved in the controversy about the incorporation if Darlington. But he did not live in Darlington and was not well known in the town, nor was he an effective speaker. It was not altogether surprising that he should be challenged by a Radical candidate, Henry King Spark.

The contest in November 1868 did not turn on policy, on which neither candidate said much: it was Spark's personal campaign against the Quaker elite. The result was a further defeat. Backhouse received 1789 votes to Spark's 872. The magnitude of Spark's defeat was a surprise. He claimed to have had 2000 signatures on the requisition to stand, and to have received 1350 firm promises of support. A show of hands on nomination day indicated that he was a much more popular candidate than Backhouse. The Sparkite newspapers denounced the unscrupulous exercise of Quaker power and the 'screw' in this battle for freedom and independence. Roughs were said to have been brought in from Middlesbrough; employers, foremen and clerks had overawed voters at every turn; members of the Pease family had been seen 'accompanying' workers as they came to record their votes. But the day of retribution would surely come, and the newspapers pledged themselves to strive for it by every means.[37]

35   *Durham Chronicle*, 8 Feb. 1867; 7 Feb., 19 Jun. 1868.
36   *Durham Chronicle*, 10 Jul. 1868; Gurney Pease diary, 18 Nov., DCRO, D/GP/11.
37   *Darlington and Stockton Times*, 21 and 28 Nov. 1868; *Darlington and Stockton Mercury*, 18 Nov.; Nossiter, *Influence, Opinion and Political Idioms*, pp. 136–40.

Accusations of improper influence were the common coin of elections, and Spark himself admitted that he might have been over-optimistic in interpreting expressions of good will as promises of support. But that some of his charges were justified was suggested by the result in Darlington in 1874, when he cut Backhouse's majority to a mere 18 votes. Contemporary explanations fastened on the intervention of a Conservative candidate, who might have cost Backhouse up to 300 votes, and on Spark's continued courting of the townspeople since 1868. The most likely explanations, however, are, first the introduction of the secret ballot which at least greatly reduced the opportunities for undue influence, and secondly the growth in the organised trade union vote of the local ironworkers' society, which went to Spark. The *Darlington and Stockton Times* claimed that Spark had won a great moral victory, 'the shackles which have hitherto bound the town hard and fast' were being laid aside, and next time Darlington would elect a really new M.P. 'Every tyranny has its day. Quakerism has had a long day. It is time it joined the Tyrannies of the past.' The *Northern Echo*, on the other hand, believed that Spark's public career was justly terminated. He was nothing but a plausible demagogue, who had done nothing for the town.[38]

In South Durham in 1874 the former Conservative candidate, Col. Charles Surtees, was not able to stand because he was high sheriff of the county. His place was taken by Lord Londonderry's eldest son Viscount Castlereagh, who was just 21 and was not taken seriously by any of the Liberals. Both Joseph Whitwell Pease and Beaumont increased the number of their votes. The Conservatives were victorious nationally, but not one Conservative candidate was returned for any seat in County Durham.[39]

In the late 1870s Liberal Party organisation developed in County Durham and Cleveland, as elsewhere in the country, with the formation of Liberal Associations and a Committee of Three Hundred in Darlington. Joseph Whitwell Pease attended meetings and encouraged the process. He also made speeches on matters such as the extension of the county franchise, and was briefly involved in a dispute with the Good Templars, who threatened to withhold support for him on temperance issues.[40] For the 1880 election Beaumont retired: in his place as second Liberal candidate appeared the Hon. Frederick Lambton, brother of the Earl of Durham. Standing in South Durham was a new departure for a Lambton, but the combination was commended by the Liberal press as likely to ensure the repetition of the Liberal triumph of 1868 and 1874. Joseph Whitwell Peases's position was now

[38]   *Darlington and Stockton Times*, 7 Feb. 1874; *Northern Echo*, 9 Mar.; Kirby, *Men of Business*, pp. 69–70; Nossiter, *Influence, Opinion and Political Idioms*, pp. 140–3.

[39]   *Durham Chronicle*, 16, 23, 30 Jan., 13 Feb. 1874; *South Durham and Cleveland Mercury*, 24 Jan.–7 Feb.; J. W. Pease diary, Jan–Feb., J. G. Pease Papers.

[40]   *Durham Chronicle*, Jun.–Sep. 1876, *passim*; 12 Jan, 1 Feb. 1877; 31 Jan, 5 Sep. 1879.

regarded as unassailable. Who was there 'in this part of the kingdom prepared to say that the Peases have not been actuated by a high sense of duty towards all the toilers by whose labours they have been enriched? There is not a speck on the family escutcheon; and there has been no more useful member of that family in the present generation than the senior representative of the Southern Division.'[41] Once again Pease increased the number of his votes, and Lambton improved on Beaumont's figure of 1874. Col. Surtees came back as Conservative candidate in place of the caretaker Castlereagh, but again came a fairly poor third.

Sir Joseph Pease enjoyed parliamentary life, more, it seems, for the position of a respected representative of his area and its interests than out of high political expectations. He was known as a useful M.P., speaking regularly on coal and railway matters, and on education, local government and the opium trade. In 1877 he brought in a private member's bill to abolish capital punishment. It seems that Sir Joseph was once offered minor governmental office but hesitated, and the opportunity did not recur. Some people thought he would have liked a peerage, but when he was sounded indirectly he left the decision to Alfred, who dropped it. That step came in the next generation.[42] Other relatives also entered Parliament in 1880. Sir Joseph's brother Arthur was invited to stand for Whitby, and got in with a good majority. Isaac Wilson had been elected for Middlesbrough in 1878 and was returned again. In Darlington there were family tensions. Henry Fell Pease was approached by some of the leading local Liberals, at the same time as Theodore Fry, husband of John Pease's daughter Sophia, was also putting himself forward. Henry Fell was doubtful about standing. This was partly for financial reasons: he reckoned that he might have to devote less time to the family woollen business but could not afford to take a cut in his salary. He also did not wish to face competition in the Committee of Three Hundred unless he could be sure of winning. There was also a feeling of resentment at Theodore Fry, who professed not to be one of the Peases, but obviously would go in on the family's influence.[43] After taking soundings in Darlington and consulting his father and cousins and David Dale, Henry Fell decided to withdraw. The choice for the Three Hundred then lay between Theodore Fry and Spark. It was understood that the one who was not selected would support the other, but when Fry was chosen Spark stood as an independent Liberal and was heavily defeated – by 2772 votes to 1331.[44] This really was the end of Spark's

41 *Durham Chronicle*, 19 Feb., 26 Mar. 1880.

42 Pease, *Wealth of Happiness*, pp. 38, 109; Notebook of Henry Kitching, c.1914, DCRO, D/Ki/303.

43 Henry Fell Pease correspondence, 1 Nov. 1879–7 Jan. 1880, DCRO, D/Pe 4/21–47.

44 *Durham Chronicle*, 16 Jan., 2 Apr. 1880; J. W. Pease diary, Feb–Apr., J. G. Pease Papers.

public career. His financial affairs were in disarray; he was finally declared bankrupt and disappeared from Darlington and from politics. On the day of the election the *Darlington and Richmond Herald* published what was in effect an obituary. Spark had never, the paper said, claimed to be a man of business. 'It is a standing marvel to all who know him that he ever managed to make any money at all, and it is the simplest thing in the world to see how he lost it.' With the help of his newspapers he was successful in self-promotion, and was said to have paid personally for the portrait that hung in the town hall. He was a ready speaker, but less attracted to hard work. Prolonged efforts to stave off bankruptcy by spinning out a settlement with Joseph Love, from whom he had borrowed money and who had bought him out of the colliery business in 1869, eventually failed. On debts of £100,000 Spark finally paid no more than one-sixth of a penny in the pound.[45] After 1880 Spark was not seen in Darlington again.

In 1884 a further measure of parliamentary reform introduced a uniform franchise for county and borough seats. The total electorate for all seats between the Tyne and the Tees was almost doubled, from 83,500 to 160,000. This time it was the county electorate that showed the greatest increase, almost quadrupling from 24,000 to 91,000. A year later redistribution of seats changed the electoral map. There were no new boroughs, but the county was now divided into eight single-member divisions, South Durham becoming the Mid-Durham, Bishop Auckland, Barnard Castle and South East Durham divisions. A new Cleveland division was created in the North Riding of Yorkshire. The combination of redistribution and an enlarged electorate necessitated changes in party organisation. In addition Liberalism was profoundly affected by divisions on Irish Home Rule and by the growth of working-class politics. Liberal party dominance in the region was no longer secure.

Sir Joseph Pease, offered the choice between three South Durham seats, chose Barnard Castle, a mixed mining and agricultural constituency. In discussing how the new seats were to be represented the *Durham Chronicle* wrote: 'For the county of Durham to be unrepresented by a member of the Pease family is what neither Liberals nor Conservatives would look for'; but the paper also warned against attempts to spread the Pease influence too far. 'Very few,' it remarked of a suggestion that David Dale might be adopted for North West Durham, 'will begrudge the great House of Pease the influence which it has won so honourably and exercised so benevolently over a great part of the county; but the parliamentary rewards of the Peases should be kept within due bounds.'[46]

The objection to Dale was not personal: as managing director of the Consett Iron Company he had good local connections and was known as a

45   *Darlington and Richmond Herald*, 3 Apr. 1880; *Northern Echo*, 2 Jun.
46   *Durham Chronicle*, 23 Jan., 24 Apr., 1 May , 8 May, 12 Jun.1885.

friend of working men; but the *Durham Chronicle* thought that his chief interests were in the railway and the south of the county, that what would be a natural claim to a seat there was being blocked by a rival claim from another member of the Pease businesses, and that either Mid or North West Durham should go to a working-class candidate. In the event William Crawford, a Lib–Lab miner, was selected for Mid Durham and Dale did not stand anywhere – his wife's health was not good. In the south of the county and north Yorkshire the bounds of the Pease influence were fairly wide. South East Durham indeed went to Sir Henry Havelock-Allan, who had his own local connections, had represented Sunderland since 1874, and could certainly not be described as part of the Pease connection despite the fact that his daughter soon afterwards married Sir Joseph's second son. Arthur Pease was defeated at Whitby in 1885 but maintained his ambitions and returned to win Darlington from Theodore Fry in 1895. He was succeeded there by his son Herbert Pike Pease. Henry Fell Pease, having withdrawn from Darlington in 1880 and having been approached about a number of Yorkshire seats, was elected for Cleveland in 1885 and sat for it until 1897. He was succeeded there by Alfred, Sir Joseph's elder son, who had represented York City between 1885 and 1892. Sir Joseph's second son Joseph Albert, generally known as Jack, turned down offers for Doncaster in 1888–9 and Houghton-le-Spring in 1891, but stood successfully for Tyneside in 1892 and remained there until 1900. Jack made a much more serious political career for himself than any other member of the family, and from an early point was advising his father about politically useful forms of local patronage, such as becoming chairman of Darlington cricket club – 'it is always advisable to keep out the Tories from patronising clubs, etc., if you can get good Liberals instead.' By the mid-1890s it was no longer safe to assume that even Sir Joseph would automatically be elected to anything he chose: in 1895 there was talk of dropping him as a candidate for North Riding County Council because he had not attended any meetings for three years. Jack advised his father to retire rather than risk defeat.[47]

In the last fifteen years of the century there were never fewer than three Peases in the House of Commons, and their relatives Theodore Fry and Isaac Wilson brought the family group up to four or five. A newspaper commented in 1897 that 'they must surely form the largest family party in the House ... Such a contingent would be well worth securing for any cause or ism if families voted *en bloc*; it is well known, however, that they carefully eschew anything like uniformity of opinion and action.'[48] Like other Liberal families the Peases became divided over Gladstone's Irish policy. In May 1886, when the first Home Rule bill was facing defeat in the House of Commons, Sir Joseph wrote to the Prime Minister begging him to withdraw it and ask for

[47]   J. A. Pease to J. W. Pease, 4 Dec. 1883, 11 Nov. 1895, Gainford Papers, 2.
[48]   *The Echo*, 1 Aug. 1897, quoted by Isichei, *Victorian Quakers*, p. 205.

time. If the bill was defeated and an election was called, 'There are many of your best supporters on the bill who would lose their seats: it is hard on them! There are others who have supported the Liberal cause for years who would retire rather than oppose their old friends in the County, who might run Home Rule candidates against them! In my own district, Darlington, a Liberal Borough is holding meetings of Liberals split into factions. At Middlesbrough the chairman of the Liberal Association is opposed to your measure.' He himself supported Home Rule but not this bill, and thought he would not be able to continue as chairman in Cleveland for Henry Fell Pease, who did vote for the bill. Alfred would probably lose his seat at York for voting in favour.[49] But Gladstone was determined to go on; the bill was defeated on second reading; and an election was called in which the Liberals lost heavily. Sir Joseph was returned unopposed in Barnard Castle, and Alfred won again at York against a combination of dissentient Liberals and Conservatives. In Darlington Theodore Fry's majority was much reduced, and whilst Sir Joseph spoke for Fry Arthur Pease insisted on speaking for the Liberal Unionist candidate. Alfred described his uncle as 'most mischievous, tearing round the county not knowing his mind.'[50] Arthur refrained from splitting the Liberal vote at Whitby, but continued to work for Liberal Unionism, as did his son Herbert Pike Pease, who upset Sir Joseph by appearing in Tory colours at a by-election in Stockton in 1888. Alfred blamed Arthur's defection on his Irish wife. He stood against Fry in Darlington in 1892 and, successfully, in 1895. On this result Sir Joseph commented: 'The first Tory Pease elected! What a come down!'[51] Herbert Pike Pease, standing as a Liberal Unionist, won the by-election in Darlington in 1898 occasioned by his father's death.

Most of the Pease colliery enterprises were situated in the Bishop Auckland and Mid Durham divisions, and their iron mining in Cleveland. All three constituencies returned Liberal M.P.s down to the First World War. Pease influence was not needed to produce this result from the miners, many of them newly enfranchised in 1884 and making up a substantial proportion of the electorate, even though Jack Pease thought in 1885 that his cousin Henry Fell would go down well with the miners, 'who have half the voting power in Cleveland, in consequence of his being a member of our firm and related to us.'[52] After 1884 probably about 55% of the miners in County Durham had the vote. It is estimated that about 1910 miners formed between 60% and 70% of the electorate in Mid Durham and North West Durham, between 50% and 60% in Chester-le-Street and Houghton-le-Spring; and

[49] J. W. Pease to Gladstone, 20 May 1886, Gladstone Papers, British Library Add. MS 44788.

[50] A. E. Pease journal, Jul. 1886, J. G. Pease Papers.

[51] *Durham Chronicle*, 25 Nov. 1887; A. E. Pease journal, Dec. 1888; J. W. Pease journal, 13 Jul. 1895, J. G. Pease Papers.

[52] J. A. Pease to J. W. Pease, 28 Apr. 1885, Gainford Papers, box 2.

between 30% and 40% in Bishop Auckland, Barnard Castle and South East Durham.[53] With such numbers, the issue in several constituencies became that of Liberal-Labour politics and working-class representation.

The Independent Labour Party was founded in 1893. For the next seven years its whole strategy was based on collaboration with the trade unions, with the aim of gaining access to trade union funds. That object was substantially achieved in 1900 with the setting up of the Labour Representation Committee. This did not mean that the bulk of the trade unions, or even of those who joined the LRC. were converted to socialism. There is little doubt that the majority of the leaders would have been content to remain in the Liberal party if the Liberals had made better provision for working-class representation; but on numerous occasions in the 1890s Liberal party constituency organisations refused to adopt working-class candidates and so pushed trade union leaders into cooperation with the ILP and into joining the LRC. This was recognised and often regretted by the national leadership of the Liberal party, but they were unable to impose a candidate on a local party.

The first miner to enter Parliament was Thomas Burt, elected in 1874 for Morpeth in Northumberland. In the 1885 election, as a result of pacts with the local Liberals, four miners were elected for Northumberland and Durham seats – Burt for Morpeth, Charles Fenwick for Wansbeck, William Crawford for Mid Durham, and John Wilson for Houghton-le-Spring. Wilson was defeated in 1886 but took over the Mid Durham seat when Crawford died, and held it until 1915. The chances of increasing the number of miner MPs depended on waiting until a seat in a mining constituency fell vacant and pressing the miners' claim on the local Liberals, or on persuading a sitting Liberal to retire and make way for a miners' candidate, or risking a three-cornered contest with the danger of letting in a Conservative. In the event, few mining seats did become vacant between 1885 and 1900, and the pressure to get sitting Liberals to retire was not great. As a result, in 1900 there were still only five miner M.P.s in the whole country.

The situation changed in 1900 with, on the one hand, the formation of the Labour Representation Committee and expansion in the number of prospective independent Labour candidates and, on the other hand, the decision of the Miners' Federation of Great Britain to set up a fund to promote candidates of its own. The union remained suspicious of the LRC, partly because its leadership was traditionally moderate and Liberal, especially in Northumberland and Durham, and partly because the concentration of mining voters was a strong argument for self-sufficiency. The union eventually joined the Labour party in 1909.

---

[53] Roy Gregory, *The Miners and British Politics 1906–1914*, Oxford 1968, pp. 12–13, 96.

The issue of independent Labour representation came to a head in Barnard Castle in 1903 with the death of Sir Joseph Pease, and was precipitated by Arthur Henderson. Henderson was an iron-moulder by trade, who had worked for some years at the Forth St. works of Robert Stephenson and Co. in Newcastle. He was an official of the Iron Founders Union, a Methodist lay preacher and a teetotaller. Henderson was elected to Newcastle city council in 1892, and was recommended as a Liberal parliamentary candidate for the city in 1895, being defeated by the Liberal Association. In the same year Henderson accepted the post of agent for Sir Joseph Pease in Barnard Castle, at a salary of £200 a year, apparently on the initiative of Jack Pease.[54] This necessitated moving to Darlington, where Henderson was elected to the town council and the county council; but he continued his trade union work. The Iron Founders Union joined the LRC from the start, and when it came to choose its first parliamentary candidate, in 1902, Henderson was top of the list.

After the Pease family business crisis in 1902 Sir Joseph offered to give up his parliamentary seat, but the Barnard Castle Liberal Association did not want to have a by-election and asked him to stay on until the next general election, probably with a known prospective successor who would share responsibility for keeping the constituency organisation going. Jack Pease, who was now M.P. for Saffron Walden, wrote to tell the Liberal Chief Whip, Herbert Gladstone, of these decisions, and added: 'At the present time Mr Arthur Henderson is agent and a fund will probably be raised to keep him in the constituency for some time to come. He, however, is obliged to give up his agency whenever he is called upon by his Trade Union to become the formal candidate for Parliament ... Some of the members are very anxious that he should appear as Labour candidate free from the trammels of any party. He is a very good Liberal and fully recognises that there are only two lobbies in the H. of C.'[55]

Henderson was adopted as Labour candidate for Barnard Castle on 1 April 1903, and was precluded by his union's membership of the LRC and his receipt of a salary from it, from standing as a Lib–Lab candidate. So far this was with an eye on the next general election: a number of other Labour candidates were being chosen at the same time for other Durham constituencies. There might have been time to sort out the conflicting

---

[54] F. M. Leventhal, *Arthur Henderson*, London 1989, p. 10; Mary Agnes Hamilton, *Arthur Henderson*, London 1938, pp. 41–5. For the 1903 by-election see also Chris Wrigley, *Arthur Henderson*, Cardiff 1990, pp. 24–34; A. W. Purdue, 'Arthur Henderson and Liberal, Liberal-Labour and Labour politics in the North East of England, 1892–1903,' in *Northern History*, 11 (1975), pp. 195–217. Hamilton's account is not wholly reliable: for example she calls Jack Pease 'Sir John.'

[55] J. A. Pease to Herbert Gladstone, BL Add. MS 46002; Purdue in *Northern History*, 11 (1975), pp. 202–03.

loyalties in Barnard Castle had not Sir Joseph Pease died on 23 June, thus bringing about a by-election. Considerable confusion followed. Henderson thought the LRC was overreaching itself in selecting candidates for Jarrow, Darlington, Sunderland and Stockton as well as Barnard Castle. He was hesitant about standing against a Liberal and would probably have preferred to go on working with Jack Pease, hoping that if the Stockton Labour candidate would stand down the Liberals would leave Barnard Castle to him. The Liberals in the North East on their side were annoyed at the proliferation of LRC candidates, and there was a Lib–Lab recovery that included the influential miner M.P.s. Although Jack Pease was personally sympathetic to Henderson, the Barnard Castle Liberals were angry at his defection and determined to put up an official candidate, Herbert Beaumont. To make matters still more confused, Beaumont came out in favour of the protectionism of the North East Liberal leader Samuel Storey, while Henderson supported the traditional Liberal policy of free trade. As one writer puts it, 'What Liberal voters in Barnard Castle had, in fact, to choose between was a candidate orthodox in name but heretical in policy and one who, though wearing the LRC label, was very close to Liberalism.'[56] The Liberal leadership, which was embarking on negotiations with Ramsay MacDonald for an electoral pact for the next general election, became hostile to Beaumont. No prominent Liberal came to speak for him; the local Liberal press was divided. Henderson made himself more acceptable to the mining vote by promising to support miner Lib–Lab candidates in future. The campaign was fought largely on the issue of tariff reform, and Henderson won with 3370 votes to the 3323 of the Conservative candidate the Hon. William Vane, and Beaumont's 2809.

Arthur Henderson was the first independent Labour M.P. to win a seat contested by both the major political parties. The by-election was complicated, as by-elections often are, by local personal issues and by the extraneous question of tariff reform. The result is probably best seen as the consequence of the failure of the Liberal party at the local level to adopt working-class candidates. So far as the Peases and their politics are concerned, whilst Jack Pease was evidently more sympathetic to Henderson than many of the Barnard Castle Liberal Association, they do not seem to have done much in the 1890s to encourage such adoptions, and it looks as though Beaumont was Sir Joseph's destined successor before his death. Some of the family moved from Liberal Unionism to Conservatism before long; others such as Alfred found themselves increasingly out of sympathy with the twentieth-century political scene. Peases continued to represent Darlington in Parliament until the 1920s, but the days of wider political influence were over.

---

[56] Purdue in *Northern History*, 11 (1975), p. 209.

CHAPTER SIX
Social and Domestic Life: Decline

To a very large extent the social lives of members of the Pease family mirror changes over the nineteenth century in the prosperous English middle class and in Quakerism that were described in Chapter One. The general trend was towards higher levels of consumption, grander houses, adoption of the leisure activities of the landed classes, marriage with non-Quakers, etc. But there was a good deal of variation in individual habits.

The fairly substantial number of diaries of members of the family that have survived, along with some correspondence, reminiscences and testimonies, convey an impression of an orderly domestic existence and a social life confined, for the most part and until late in the century, to exchanges of family and neighbourly entertainment. There were no black sheep and no eccentrics. Members of the family travelled abroad, first for religious purposes, later for pleasure; but life at home seems to have remained ordinary and undramatic, with a strong continuing thread of public service and good works. The diaries, however, lack comment on events and on most feelings (except religious ones), and are at times a disappointing source.

Edward Pease remained a plain Friend until his death on 31 July 1858 at the age of ninety-one. He never gave up Quaker dress and speech; his domestic life was comfortable but unassuming. As a young man he enjoyed fishing and shooting, and light reading (which one suspects was not very light by other than evangelical standards), but gave them up as he settled into married life and business.[1] He married, in 1796, Rachel Whitwell of Kendal and two years later moved into a plain three-storied town house in Northgate. At that time it was the last house on the road out of the centre of Darlington, but soon there was more building beyond it. There was a large garden running down to the Skerne, containing the largest acacia tree in the town, and many fruit trees – peaches, nectarines, cherries, apricots, plums, pears and several varieties of apple.[2] After his beloved wife's death in 1833 Edward Pease spent a good deal of time with his married daughters in Bristol and Saffron Walden, and accompanied his son John or his cousin Hannah Backhouse on their religious journeys. When members of the family came to dinner with

[1]   *Diaries of Edward Pease*, pp. 48-9. See the biographical sketch by the editor, Sir A. E. Pease.
[2]   *Op. cit.*, App. VI.

him in Darlington they continued to wear Quaker dress even after the younger ones had given it up for everyday use. Edward kept an excellent table, with good quality linen, china, silver and glass. He was not a teetotaller: beer was always provided; and after the white table cloth was removed heavy cut glass decanters of madeira, port, and two other kinds of Portuguese wine were put on the table with the fruit from the garden that formed the dessert.[3]

Edward Pease was scrupulous about worldly amusements, even what others might have regarded as innocent. For example in the summer of 1834 he lent the use of a field next to his house for a balloon launch, but worried about his moral responsibility in case of an accident.[4] Although a keen gardener, he worried about the display and social doings connected with the Darlington Horticultural Society and his own family's involvement.[5] He was never wholly reconciled to two of his sons standing for Parliament. He was frequently troubled about his sons' preoccupation with business and about their spending on houses.[6] Edward was constantly mindful of the obligation on himself and his family to use their increasing wealth for the good of others.[7] The prospect of the development of Cleveland iron ore filled him with anxiety 'that none of my beloved family may be caught in its enticings: they have quite enough of this world's engagements ... Whether it succeeds or disappoints, its consequences are to be dreaded.'[8] Edward did not care for the way his eldest grandson's twenty-first birthday was celebrated: 'I can rejoice in the happiness and comfort of my townspeople, but the celebration so large and so public of anything pertaining to my family pains me, being beyond the simplicity of Gospel limits according to my feelings.'[9] Whilst continuing to take an interest in the achievements of railway and mining development, Edward did not like public dinners for such occasions, or his sons participating in celebrations that involved 'the drinking of healths and toasts which is followed often by unmeaning speeches and those maddening huzzas which better become the Lunatick than the man of sober sense, etc.'[10]

Edward Pease's dislike of junketings and huzzas did not preclude generosity to the family's employees, as for example a large tea meeting to celebrate the rebuilding of the Priestgate woollen mills in 1857 when he gave a shilling to everyone who came.[11] He regularly gave presents to the children at

[3]   *Op. cit.*, p. 145.
[4]   *Op. cit.*, p. 71; Richardson, *Local Historian's Table Book*, Vol. 4, p. 200.
[5]   *Diaries of Edward Pease*, pp. 246, 260; Longstaffe, *History and Antiquities of Darlington*, p. 325. Joseph Pease was one of the first secretaries of the society.
[6]   *Diaries of Edward Pease*, pp. 214, 231–2, 238–9, 242.
[7]   E.g. *Diaries of Edward Pease*, pp. 147, 151–2, 160–1.
[8]   *Op. cit.*, p. 299.
[9]   *Op. cit.*, pp. 270–1.
[10] *Op. cit.*, pp. 188, 199, 212, 337.
[11] *Darlington and Stockton Times*, 5 Feb. 1857.

the school at Great Ayton which he had helped to found. One of his last acts was to go to the school's 1858 annual meeting, giving each child a little present, and coming home cheerfully remarking that he thought they had never done better.[12] A year earlier, when Edward reached the age of ninety, some Darlington citizens led by his old friend Francis Mewburn, got up a movement to promote a memorial and perhaps a statue. Edward had in 1848 'very reluctantly' agreed to have his portrait painted. Now, on being consulted, he vetoed a memorial; but since a strong feeling remained that something must be done to mark the occasion, a congratulatory address was presented to him in a modest ceremony at his house.[13]

Edward Pease's spiritual reflections fit into the Quaker discipline of regular self-examination. They were often anxious and gloomy until his last years, when he felt more assured; but his family and others remembered him as a cheerful man, accessible and generous, his society attractive to the young. As a businessman he was, according to the tributes uttered on his death, thoughtful, shrewd and resourceful, owing his success to farsightedness, determination, and unremitting attention to detail. He was said to 'worship cent per cent,' and to have pursued profit at all times, 'never losing sight of the main chance and always buying in the cheapest market to sell in the dearest market.' But his enemies never questioned his integrity, and he was said never to have used underhand methods to gain his ends.[14] All the shops in Darlington were closed for the funeral.[15]

Edward Pease's sons departed in his lifetime from his austere attitude to the world, and over the next fifty years further adaptations were made to changing social conditions. One of these changes was in houses. When he moved into it, Edward Pease's house in Northgate was on the edge of Darlington but a town house in style. By the time he died the north and east side of the town had become hemmed in by the railway lines and industry, and the houses of the business and professional classes were spreading to the south and west. Many of them were owned by Quakers. 'The leading families of the Friends,' wrote a local historian in 1854, 'have made their fortunes with their own right hands, and have settled down in all the best and snuggest

12 Society of Friends, *Annual Monitor*, 1859, pp. 122–6; F. Mewburn diary, DCRO, D/XD/24/2, pp. 283–4.

13 *Diaries of Edward Pease*, pp. 232, 347; Mewburn, *Memoir of Fra: Mewburn*, pp. 59–60; Mewburn, *Larchfield Diary*, p. 144; testimonial, DCRO, D/Ho/F/94 (1); *Northern Daily Express*, 21 Feb. 1857; *Durham Chronicle*, 6 Mar., 30 Oct.; *Darlington and Stockton Times*, 24 Oct., Joseph Pease diary, 4 Mar., J. G. Pease Papers. Edward thought the address 'quite too full and above all our services.'

14 *Diaries of Edward Pease*, p. 109; *Durham Chronicle*, 6 Aug. 1858; *Illustrated London News*, 7 Aug.; Mewburn, *Memoir of Fra: Mewburn*, pp. 60–3.

15 J. W. Pease diary, 5 Aug. 1858, J. G. Pease Papers; *Darlington and Stockton Times*, 7 Aug.

mansions near the town. They have ample gardens and green plantations, plain houses and high walls, and there is an air of the quintessence of comfort in their grounds.' And again, 'Their grounds are enviable places of solace and retirement, where they allow the Horticultural Society's meetings to be held.'[16] Twenty years later the author of *Kings of British Commerce* marked a further stage: 'Westward and southward ever-advancing lines of villas bear the surest testimony to the presence of a substantial middle class. Here and there these lines of villas are interrupted by the spacious grounds and handsome residences of some wealthy Quakers. Some of these residences are palatial in their extent and beauty.'[17] Three-quarters of them belonged to members of the Pease family.

The house belonging to Joseph Pease whose embellishment Edward criticised was Southend which he bought, from Jonathan Backhouse, on his marriage in 1826. At that time it was on the south-west edge of the town. Joseph probably added a third storey and a nursery extension, as well as a portico entrance and monumental features. Joseph also added to the grounds over the years, and they eventually extended to twenty-seven acres, with five summer houses, two fountains, a conservatory with a cage full of canaries, an arbour, hothouses and kitchen gardens. The terrace was gravelled with purple and white fluorspar from Weardale, which gave it the appearance of a sheet of amethyst and crystal.[18] Many of the Peases loved gardens. Joseph was devoted to his, finding it a refreshment in times of business stress; and later his grandchildren found it an excellent playground. Joseph also built a house at Marske-by-the-Sea as a summer home for his family. Not long after he moved into Southend his elder brother John built himself a house, called East Mount, across the Skerne from his father's gardens, and lived there until his death in 1868, adding to it from time to time.[19] Also on the north side of Darlington, opposite Edward Pease's house, was North Lodge, built by John Beaumont Pease, son of Joseph Pease of Feethams, on land bought from the Backhouse estate of Elmfield. North Lodge was a fairly plain two-storey house with gardens behind.[20]

The brother with the showiest house and largest gardens was Henry. Pierremont, which he bought in 1845, was the first large Darlington house to be built in the Gothic style. It was referred to as the 'Buckingham Palace of Darlington,' and Henry as the 'Laird of Pierremont.' Henry added to the house and in 1873 had it substantially enlarged to designs by Alfred Waterhouse, a successful architect of Quaker origins and Darlington

[16]   Longstaffe, *History and Antiquities of Darlington*, pp. 252, 336.
[17]   *Kings of British Commerce*, p. 49.
[18]   Vera Chapman, *Rural Darlington. Farm, Mansion and Suburb*, Durham 1975, pp. 30, 44; Sir A. E. Pease, 'Autobiographical record,' J. G. Pease Papers.
[19]   *Diaries of Edward Pease*, p. 212; Chapman, *Rural Darlington*, p. 49.
[20]   Chapman, *Rural Darlington*, p. 48.

connections, who was responsible for, among other public buildings, the Natural History Museum in London and Manchester Town Hall. To Pierremont Waterhouse added a large conservatory, a new bay to the dining room and the bedroom above it, and extra bedrooms over the domestic quarters. The grounds extended to twenty-eight acres, with a fish pond and an ice house, terraces and a sunken garden. Henry also bought land the other side of the road and developed a boggy field into Pierremont South Park, which had trees, an ornamental lake, a grotto, waterfall and twenty-foot-high fountain, a rose-pergola promenade, and a 'Swiss cottage' for the gardener. The park was open to the public, and the visitors book contained names from all over the country and abroad. Henry also planted trees along the roads into the town. After his second marriage and a new family he had a house at Saltburn for the summer, and acquired Stanhope Castle in Weardale. It had been empty for some years, and Henry enjoyed doing it up and, especially, reconstructing the gardens.[21]

The next generation saw the first major branching out in houses. Joseph Whitwell Pease married in 1854 Mary Fox, daughter of a Falmouth Quaker family of shipping agents. The young couple lived first at Woodlands, an 1820s house on the west side of Darlington, with a park large enough to keep cows in. In 1860 Joseph Whitwell had the house enlarged to accommodate his growing family, adding a bay to the drawing room, spacious domestic quarters, and nurseries, a bathroom, and servants' bedrooms upstairs, and a tower.[22] Then in 1867 he and his family moved to Hutton Hall, near Guisborough. The old house, which had been rented for some years as a summer home, was pulled down and a new one built by Waterhouse. It was large, red brick, with steep gables. It had six reception rooms, forty bed and dressing rooms, and five bathrooms. There was stabling for twenty-four horses, a conservatory and winter garden, and large gardens with ten green-houses, all set in private grounds of fifty-four acres and an estate of nearly 300 acres on the north face of the Cleveland Hills under Roseberry Topping. Together with neighbouring Pinchinthorpe and Nunthorpe, which Joseph Whitwell also bought, the combined estate amounted to nearly 3000 acres.[23] Pinchinthorpe, which became the home of Alfred on his marriage, was a comparatively modest-sized house with twelve bedrooms. Nunthorpe was acquired in 1897 from Isaac Wilson and was done up for Jack and his wife at a cost of £16,000. It had twenty-seven bedrooms, four reception rooms, and stabling for seventeen horses. At Hutton Joseph Whitwell set up as a landed gentleman, the first of his family to do so, and brought up his children in like

[21] *Diaries of Edward Pease*, p. 217; Chapman, *Rural Darlington*, pp. 30, 35, 50–2; Mary H. Pease, *Henry Pease, A Short Story of his Life*, London 1897.

[22] Chapman, *Rural Darlington*, p. 47; A. E. Pease, 'Autobiographical record,' J. G. Pease Papers.

[23] Pease, *Wealth of Happiness*, pp. 2–6.

style. He also had a house at Falmouth, his wife's home, and one in London for his parliamentary duties.

Three of Joseph Pease's sons moved, on getting married, into new houses built in the Peases' own white brick. Edward and Gurney had a pair of Gothic semi-detached houses, reminiscent of Abbotsford, called East and West Green- croft on the west side of Darlington. Arthur, the third son, set up house at Hummersknott, a little farther out. He laid out a splendid park with avenues and carriage drives, and lent it for the railway jubilee celebrations in 1875 and for agricultural shows including the Royal Show in 1895 which attracted over 100,000 visitors.[24] The Hummersknott grounds eventually covered over 260 acres with farms and other houses, more like a country estate than the large grounds of a big suburban house.

The 1860s were something of a peak period in house-building. In addition to Hutton Hall, Greencroft and Hummersknott, Brinkburn was built on land near Pierremont by Henry Fell Pease, Henry's eldest son, when he married his cousin Elizabeth, daughter of John Beaumont Pease. Unusually, this house was of stone, with a slate roof. The gardens and grounds eventually covered what had been nine fields. A few years later John Pease of East Mount built two houses outside the town for his daughters. Woodburn was given to Sophia, who married Theodore Fry; Elm Ridge was meant for John himself, his wife and his second daughter Mary Anna; but John died before he could move in, and his wife shortly afterwards. Mary Anna married in 1873 and Elm Ridge became home to her Hodgkin family for over fifty years.[25] John Beaumont Pease bought a house and land outside Darlington on the Staindrop road. His son Edwin Lucas went to live there in the 1870s, and in 1881 demolished the house and rebuilt it as Mowden Hall, in bright red brick with sandstone dressings and red tiled roof, many gables, big oriels, and an elaborate Gothic portico.[26]

In these large houses and extensive grounds the Peases continued to live as Quakers. No member of the family resigned from the Society of Friends before the end of the century: all were regular in attendance at meeting for worship. Some were more active than others. Edward Pease's eldest son John was recorded as a minister at the age of twenty-five and travelled extensively. He was given a certificate to travel by Darlington monthly meeting on no fewer than forty-six occasions. He spent two years in the United States in the 1840s, and visited France and Germany as well as most parts of the United Kingdom. He was a notable preacher, at home and abroad.[27] Joseph's time was

---

[24] Chapman, *Rural Darlington*, pp. 49–50, 56–8; *Durham Chronicle*, 3 Apr. 1877.

[25] Chapman, *Rural Darlington*, pp. 52, 55–6.

[26] *Op. cit.*, p. 58.

[27] Testimonies on John and Sophia Pease, 15 Dec. 1868, 20 Dec. 1870, Darlington Monthly Meeting minutes, DCRO, SF/Da/MM 1/12; Society of Friends, *Annual Monitor*, 1869, pp. 114–35.

necessarily mainly devoted to business. He sometimes worried that this distracted his mind too much, but consoled himself with the thought that public as well as private good might result from his efforts.[28] When his eldest son came of age in 1849 Joseph asked the workers assembled at Adelaide colliery to 'unite with me in humble desires – in prayers – that ... he may fulfil his duties, by the help of God, as a true Christian and true patriot; that his ear may never be deaf to the complaint of the poor or the tale of woe; that he may be willing, to the best of his powers, to discharge his duties in the sight of God and of his fellow-creatures, and that he will bring "all things" and lay them upon the altar of Him that gave them; remembering that he, and you, and I must look for the only lasting inheritance beyond the grave.'[29] As long as Joseph lived the family used plain speech in his presence; and he was upset when his son Gurney, still living at home unmarried, abandoned Quaker dress for evening wear. Joseph feared that this meant a casting off of parental authority, but Gurney tried to explain that he had long felt that any particular garb was not necessary, and that in continuing to wear this one in the evening he was acting inconsistently if not hypocritically. Gurney hoped all the same to be 'kept in all Christian simplicity' and assured his father that he welcomed 'the parental care that has always been so lovingly extended.'[30] As for Joseph's own spiritual standing as a Christian businessman, the *Friends Quarterly Examiner* must have heard some doubts expressed, for it commented after his death: 'It is probably as difficult for all mere onlookers to say what is or is not the duty of a Christian so immersed in things, upon the continuous working of which whole districts depend, as it would be for them to offer an opinion upon the affairs themselves. We believe that the only test which can be applied to those upon whom the success of whose designs the prosperity of half a county is more or less dependent, is not whether the business ramifications be too vast for one mind to grapple with and control, but whether, whilst so occupied as a Christian capitalist, he lives as a man striving for a higher country, and with his face set fixedly upon a nobler goal; ever watchful not to become entangled with the cares of the world, and not to overcharge himself with trade or other outward engagements to the hindrance of religious progress.'[31]

Henry Pease was an elder for many years, and although he gave up Quaker dress, he continued to use plain speech into the 1860s. It was only in his last years that he allowed a piano at Pierremont, and he continued to disapprove of dancing, hoping in 1877 that his son and daughter-in-law would not attend the mayor's ball in Darlington.[32] Henry also objected to a theatre

[28] E.g. Joseph Pease diary, 6 Oct. 1827, 3 May 1828, J. G. Pease Papers.
[29] Reid, *Middlesbrough and its Jubilee*, pp. 166–7.
[30] Gurney Pease diary, 8 Mar. 1860; Gurney Pease to Joseph Pease, 8 Mar., DCRO, D/GP/3, D/XD 64/1/9.
[31] *Friends Quarterly Examiner*, 6 (1872), pp. 157–72.

in Darlington. The increasing emphasis on temperance among Quakers in the second half of the century is reflected in the Pease family. Henry was not a teetotaller but supported the temperance cause for social reasons; Joseph was not a teetotaller, but several of his children were, as was his cousin John Beaumont Pease. John Beaumont, however, also abhorred intolerance and sectarianism, thinking rather of the whole Christian world as 'one great family worshipping the Almighty in different ways according to their separate methods.'[33]

Joseph Pease's daughters Jane and Emma, who did not marry, lived on at Southend after his death: they made the household teetotal, and maintained the practice of 'family reading,' with Bible reading and prayer, with the servants. Jane always wore Quaker dress for meeting and refrained, out of scruple about causing difficulty to Friends of tender conscience, from sharing in religious service outside the Society. This position, by the 1890s, was regretted by the *Annual Monitor*, which remarked that it stood in the way of the activity in philanthropic and educational work that was now characteristic of Quakerism. 'Growing up in the shelter of a very favoured home, without those resources in active work for the benefit of others which now call so many to labour who desire to serve the Lord, free from all domestic cares and anxieties, the state of her own spiritual health naturally absorbed a great deal of her attention.'[34] Jane's brother Arthur, on the other hand, felt able to take part in, and occasionally to conduct, services at mission rooms and chapels of other denominations.[35]

Gurney Pease, his brother Charles, and his cousin Henry Fell, all as young bachelors living at home, taught in First Day schools. Gurney also ran a Bible class for iron workers. His diaries often reveal feelings of inadequacy about his teaching, and complain of poor attendance and lack of results; but pupils later expressed appreciation Henry Fell ran a Bible class for railway workers for many years. He continued to use plain speech to his father in the 1860s, and to use the Quaker style for days of the week and months, but when away from home quite often went to church if no meeting was available.[36] Causes with which Quakers were particularly associated, such as peace, anti-slavery and anti-opium trade, were supported more or less actively by most members of the family, although none was called to repeat Henry's

[32]   Henry Pease to Henry Fell and Elizabeth Pease, 20 Jan. 1877, DCRO, D/Pe 2/63.
[33]   Memoranda read to relatives on the evening of John Beaumont Pease's funeral, 18 Nov. 1873, DCRO, D/Pe 1/79.
[34]   Society of Friends, *Annual Monitor*, 1895, pp. 130–47.
[35]   Darlington Monthly Meeting minutes, Jan. 1899, DCRO, SF/Da/MM 1/19; *Annual Monitor*, 1899, pp. 86–97.
[36]   E.g. Gurney Pease diaries, 1 Apr. 1860, DCRO, D/GP/4; Darlington Monthly Meeting minutes, 18 Jul. 1872 SF/Da/MM 1/13; *Annual Monitor*, 1874, pp. 157–62; Henry Fell Pease diaries, 1860, 1861, 1862, D/Pe 5, 16, 19.

visit to Russia of 1854. Sir Joseph enjoyed reading military history, and gave tacit support to the government's policy in the Boer War; but he threatened to alter his will when his eldest grandson tried to enlist.[37] Alfred extracted his son from this situation, but for himself declined to follow his father in the presidency of the Peace Society. Jack accepted, but resigned in 1914. In the First War several members of the family served in the armed forces as a matter of course.

In addition to participating in public bodies and social organisations, members of the family exercised personal philanthropy over a wide range. Joseph Pease's grandson, years later destroying a large quantity of his correspondence, remarked on the variety of his philanthropic interests. In the year 1869, for example, Joseph was giving large sums of money to Allonby almshouses, the Cotherstone Friends, and Clarkson's publishing house. He was financing the publication of a Spanish translation of Jonathan Dymond's *Principles of Morality* (for which the Spanish government gave him a medal), supporting an eye hospital (he had gone blind with glaucoma), giving a fire engine to Darlington, and bestowing microscopes and telescopes on any school he heard of. He paid for building a Quaker meeting house at Redcar and several in the United States, helped impoverished Friends and individuals in distress, gave Cotherstone cheeses by the score as presents, and conducted an extensive correspondence about good causes.[38]

In Quakerism women were theoretically equal to men. They could be ministers, and in the early Victorian period a majority of ministers were in fact women. This was strikingly different from the position accorded to women in other churches, or for that matter in secular society, and made a great impression on contemporaries. In practice, apart from this important opportunity women had little say in Quaker organisation and decision-making until late in the century.[39] The ministry gave notable women such as Elizabeth Fry an opening which they could exploit in furthering social causes; but on the whole Quaker women seem to have occupied much the same position as their non-Quaker contemporaries in family and social life. In Darlington, in the first half of the century there were two prominent women ministers. Hannah Chapman Backhouse was married to a cousin of Edward Pease, and her sister Emma married Joseph. Sophia Jowitt, John Pease's wife, accompanied him on some of his religious journeys as well as ministering in her own right. John Beaumont Pease's sister Elizabeth was active, with her father, in the anti-slavery movement. She married a fellow campaigner and Glasgow university professor John Pringle Nichol. Since he was not a Quaker and the marriage rule had not yet been relaxed, Elizabeth was disowned – a

---

[37] A. E. Pease journal, 18 Dec. 1900, J. G. Pease Papers; Isichei, *Victorian Quakers*, p. 151.

[38] A. E. Pease journal, 19 Feb. 1909, J. G. Pease Papers.

[39] Isichei, *Victorian Quakers*, pp. 94–5, 107–09.

good example of the kind of loss to the Society of Friends that John Stephenson Rowntree deplored.[40] Most other women members of the Pease family took part in local philanthropic work of one kind or another. To take a few examples, Joseph Pease's daughter Jane subscribed to the building of a new mechanics' institute and laid its foundation stone in 1853. Her sister Emma served on the committee of a charity that helped poor families with linen, etc. on the birth of a child.[41] Their cousin Sophia, John Pease's daughter, was active from girlhood in educational causes: she also raised money for the new general hospital and for years ran a 'mothers' meeting,' a non-sectarian combination of savings club, burial club and self-improvement society for women.[42] Henry Pease's second wife Mary Lloyd was for nearly thirty years secretary of the convalescent home at Redcar, founded and ran a mothers' meeting at Cockerton for over forty years, and served on the committee of the training college. Henry Fell Pease's wife Elizabeth taught in First Day schools, ran a clothing club, and wrote Scripture notes for her husband's Bible class and a temperance pamphlet.[43] In the home, many of the women taught their young children and less young daughters themselves.

From their beginning Quakers set great store by family life and the upbringing of children. Epistles from the Yearly Meeting abound almost annually with references to the importance of early teaching, parents setting a good example, training children for heaven as well as earth, and so on, but also to treating them gently, showing sympathy and entering into their interests. Diaries and letters of members of the Pease family are full of unforced and obviously genuine affection. Edward Pease, for example, constantly referred to his 'dear sons,' mourned the deaths of two sons and a daughter, thought lovingly of his dead wife, wrote charming letters to young grandchildren, and showed the most tender sensitivity to one son who was depressed and unwell after some business setback: 'If thou feels a little cast down with cares come over here to refresh and rest, never mind business for a few days. Thy dear Mother does not know I am thus writing but thou canst be sure she and we all will be glad to have thee.'[44] Joseph read hymns with his children every day after breakfast, spent time with them when he came home from business in the evening, and expressed pleasure in their company. Boys were sent to Quaker boarding schools, in York or Tottenham, about the age of eight. There was a Quaker girls' school in Darlington, founded in 1848; but

[40] Anna M. Stoddart, *Saintly Lives. Elizabeth Pease Nichol*, London 1899.
[41] *Durham Chronicle*, 18 Apr. 1851; Fordyce, *History and Antiquities of Durham*, pp. 475–6; Report of Darlington Maternity Charity, 1889, DCRO, D/XD/10/6.
[42] Eliza Orme, *Lady Fry of Darlington*, London 1898.
[43] Chapman, *Rural Darlington*, pp. 45–6; Elizabeth Pease diary, 1859, DCRO, D/Pe 5/42; correspondence, 1890–94, D/Pe 6/47–74; 'E.F.P.', *Thoughts in Quiet Hours*, London 1890.
[44] Edward Pease to Edward Pease jr, 2 Mar. 1830, DCRO, D/Pe 2/9.

it is not certain whether any of the Pease daughters attended it.[45] Alfred and Jack Pease were the first members of the family to go to university. Before 1871, when religious tests were dropped, none of them could have gone to Oxford or Cambridge. London University never had tests, but the older generation of Quakers went straight into business on leaving school.

In the home, plentiful provision was made for human appetite and comfort. At Southend, the daily routine of meals was a large breakfast at 8.30 am, dinner at 1.30 or 2 pm, afternoon tea at 4.30, 'meat tea' at 6.30, and supper at 8.30 pm. Family dinners on Sundays consisted of roast beef followed by four kinds of sweets and a Stilton or Cotherstone cheese. On weekdays dessert was a great feature, with pineapples, nectarines, peaches, grapes, figs and melons, all grown in the garden. Joseph and Joseph Whitwell alone drank wine, the latter with seltzer water. On Sundays the grandchildren used red glass Dresden mugs.[46]

Major family occasions, weddings and comings of age, were causes for celebration, sometimes ostentatious. Edward Pease, as has been seen, did not like the scale of the festivities for Joseph Whitwell's coming of age in 1849. Some 150 employees were entertained to tea at Southend, about 300 of the women and girls from the mill to tea at the Central Hall; and there was a cold meal and dinner for some 1700 men at the Adelaide pit, with Joseph and his whole family present. Francis Mewburn found the participation of bands and the ringing of bells 'singular' for a Quaker celebration.[47] Two years later, when Joseph's daughter Rachel married Charles Leatham, there was more bell-ringing, the Central Hall brass band paraded the streets, flags were flown on the stations of the Stockton and Darlington railway, and – 'curious' in Mewburn's opinion – there were salvoes of artillery. The bride was attended to the meeting house by seven bridesmaids.[48] On the other hand the marriage in 1857 of Joseph Pease's youngest daughter Elizabeth Lucy to John Fowler seems to have been celebrated only with a family tea after the 'solemn and good' meeting; and in Kendal the Wilson family celebrated their daughter Katherine's wedding to Gurney Pease in 1863 fairly quietly, with about sixty-four people sitting down to a meal after the meeting.[49] A much grander celebration marked the wedding in Darlington of John Beaumont Pease's daughter Elizabeth to her cousin Henry Fell Pease. The meeting house was crammed, hundreds of onlookers stood outside, flags were flown, church bells rang at intervals throughout the day. The wedding reception at North Lodge was on a magnificent scale, the great variety of soups, pies, aspics, creams,

[45]   Chapman, *Rural Darlington*, pp. 39–40.
[46]   A. E. Pease journal, 19 May 1882; 'Autobiographical record,' J. G. Pease Papers.
[47]   *Diaries of Edward Pease*, pp. 270–1; Mewburn, *Larchfield Diary*, p. 99.
[48]   *Darlington and Stockton Times*, 6 Mar. 1851; Mewburn, *Larchfield Diary*, p. 106.
[49]   Joseph Pease diary, 30 Jul. 1857, J. G. Pease Papers; Gurney Pease diary, 23 Apr. 1863, DCRO, D/GP/6.

pastries, fruits and ices carefully listed by the local paper; but the accompanying liquid refreshment in that teetotal household was soda water, lemon water, and temperance champagne. The staff at North Lodge were given a supper after their exertions; Henry Pease gave the employees at Stanhope Castle a dinner; and on the day after the wedding 700 of the workers at the woollen mills were given an excursion by rail to Redcar, accompanied by a sax-horn band and with a tip of 1s. or 2s. for each person.[50]

Joseph Whitwell Pease also marked his children's comings of age and marriages in style. When Alfred came of age in 1878 department heads from the various branches of the family businesses, farm tenants and dozens of relatives – some 800 people in all – were brought to Hutton by special train, and there was another celebration two days later.[51] Two years later Alfred's sister Emma married a non-Quaker in Guisborough parish church. In addition to a reception for family and friends, the principal residents and tradesmen of the town were invited to a celebration, with tea and fireworks and other entertainments, in a specially constructed wooden building put up near Hutton Lowcross school. The catering was done by Mrs Hancroft, who ran the station dining rooms at Middlesbrough.[52] Alfred and Jack both married non-Quakers. Alfred's wife Helen (Nellie) Fowler was a cousin but her father had resigned from the Society of Friends and she was brought up an Anglican. Jack married Elsie Havelock-Allan, daughter of a general who had won the Victoria Cross at the siege of Lucknow and who looked down on the Peases as tradesmen.[53]

Sir Joseph Pease continued to describe himself as belonging to the business class, but by the 1880s his and his family's life-style were far removed from that of his grandfather. From the time of his first election to parliament in 1865 his life followed an almost unvarying pattern. The first half of the year was spent mainly in London, with frequent weekend trips north; the summer and autumn were divided between Hutton, Scotland, and holidays abroad. To take one fairly typical year, 1886, as an example, the first ten days of January were spent at Hutton, with business and constituency affairs taking up a good deal of time; mid-January to Easter in London, with several weekends at Darlington; Easter at Hutton. Parliament was dissolved early in June, and whilst Sir Joseph himself was not opposed at Barnard Castle he spent several weeks electioneering for his brother Arthur at Whitby and his cousin Sophia's husband Theodore Fry at Darlington. Five weeks in August and September were passed in Switzerland, and much of the autumn at Hutton broken by ten days shooting in Scotland.[54] By the 1890s the Society of

50 *Darlington and Stockton Times*, 17 May 1862.
51 Pease, *Wealth of Happiness*, pp. 11–12.
52 A. E. Pease journal, Nov. 1880, J. G. Pease Papers.
53 Pease, *Wealth of Happiness*, pp. 64–5.
54 J. W. Pease diary, 1886, J. G. Pease Papers.

Friends had given up detailed criticism of forms of recreation, leaving it to individuals to consider their responsibility. Well before this Sir Joseph took to hunting and shooting, sea fishing, and deer stalking. His sons hunted regularly and with enthusiasm. Other members of the family were less devoted to field sports. Gurney neither hunted nor shot; Henry's family and guests at Stanhope shot on the moors, but it does not seem that Henry himself took part; Henry Fell shot six or seven times a year, but was evidently not especially keen. It seems that it was only Sir Joseph and his immediate family who took whole-heartedly to the sporting activities of the landed gentry.

By the time they did so the years of business expansion were over. Joseph Pease's death in 1872 virtually coincided with the onset of a long period of industrial and commercial uncertainty. Coal fetched unprecedently high prices in 1873–4 and then fell heavily. Prices did not begin to recover until 1890 and then fluctuated before picking up at the end of the decade. For a number of years in the 1880s and '90s Pease and Partners paid no dividend.[55] The iron trade, on which the Peases' coke business largely depended, slumped in the mid 1870s, sending a number of Cleveland firms out of business. Overall the iron and steel trade was subject for some years to violent fluctuations in output, prices and profit.[56] The fortunes of the North Eastern Railway reflected those of the regional economy. Gross revenue boomed until 1873 and then fluctuated for twenty years before recovering well from 1895.[57]

In addition to the difficulties of the coal and iron trades, two enterprises in which the Peases had substantial stakes but which they did not manage, faced problems in the 1880s and 90s that caused them personal financial loss and put a strain on the banking branch. After the premature death of Robert Stephenson in 1859 the successful locomotive-building and engineering firm in Newcastle that bore his name seems to have lost momentum, and failed to meet foreign competition. Edward Pease had put up about half the original capital and was a partner. Joseph Pease also became a partner and left a large interest in the firm to his sons; but throughout the management was entirely in the hands of the Stephenson family. In 1886 the firm was converted into a private limited company, with just under half the shares held by Sir Joseph and Arthur Pease. But although their obligations as partners were now limited, the firm continued to lose money. By 1899 accumulated losses amounted to over £500,000, and nearly one third of the total was debited to the private accounts of Sir Joseph and Arthur Pease at J. and J. W. Pease.[58]

[55] Church, *Coal Industry*, Vol. 3, pp. 3, 54, 58–9; Pease, *Wealth of Happiness*, pp. 30, 50, 69, 115.

[56] Carr and Taplin, *History of the British Steel Industry*, pp. 38, 83–4, 94–7, 104–08, 123–30.

[57] R. J. Irving, *The North Eastern Railway Company 1870–1914. An Economic History*, Leicester 1976, pp. 21–41, 155, 292; Kirby, *Men of Business*, pp. 73–6.

[58] 'The affairs of J. and J. W. Pease,' Ruskin College, Gainford Papers [125]; Kirby,

The second firm to cause difficulty was Wilsons, Pease and Co. This was the successor to the engine works and iron foundry established at Middlesbrough in 1843 by Edgar Gilkes, Isaac Wilson and Charles Leatham. Joseph Beaumont Pease, grandson of Joseph Pease of Feethams and son-in-law of Isaac Wilson, became a partner in the firm, and after his death in 1873 his share passed to Sir Joseph. The firm banked with J. and J. W. Pease, but was managed entirely by members of the Wilson family. In the iron recession of 1879–81 Sir Joseph put a good deal of his own money into the company. It survived, but losses mounted. By 1901 it had accumulated an overdraft of over £150,000 at the bank; and its plant, equipment and management needed modernisation.[59]

A further cause for concern was the family's own original woollen business, Henry Pease and Co. After the reorganisation in the 1850s it was managed successively by Henry, Edward (briefly) and Henry Fell Pease, but it was not profitable. The problem was not technological obsolescence. In the early 1870s buildings were refurbished and new equipment installed; in 1894 the Priestgate mills were rebuilt after a fire. Even so, the firm lost money, at an average of £7000 a year in the 1870s. In 1882, when the colliery, ironstone and limestone department were combined into Pease and Partners, it was decided to run Henry Pease and Co. only at the lowest level consistent with keeping the mills going. Alfred favoured closing the firm down, but instead it was leased and continued to need injections of money. Sir Joseph extended credit from his own account at the bank to the amount of over £100,000; but even with this assistance the firm's overdraft came in 1902 to £140,000.[60]

Not only did Sir Joseph put large sums of money from his own account into these loss-making Pease-related enterprises, he also gave help to several unrelated Middlesbrough ironmasters in the collapse of the late 1870s. He and Arthur Pease gave help to relatives in need of credit. Sir Joseph absorbed losses made by the *Northern Echo*, a newspaper set up in 1870 on the initiative of a Pease-led group of Liberals to counter Spark's *Darlington and Stockton Times*: Alfred Pease was a director from 1887 to 1895, when the paper was sold.[61] Sir Joseph also took personal responsibility for losses made by J. W. Pease and Co., the ironstone and limestone department, in the 1870s before the reorganisation into Pease and Partners. He spent large sums of his own money on properties in Darlington owned by the family.

    Men of Business, p. 79.

59   Kirby, *Men of Business*, pp. 79–80.

60   Pease, *Wealth of Happiness*, pp. 19, 21, 32, 60; Kirby, *Men of Business*, p. 80.

61   Maurice Milne, *The Newspapers of Northumberland and Durham. A Study of their Progress during the 'Golden Age' of the Provincial Press*, Newcastle upon Tyne 1971, pp. 87–93; Alan J. Lee, *The Origins of the Popular Press in England 1855–1914*, London 1976, pp. 136, 175; Pease, *Wealth of Happiness*, pp. 51, 62, 115.

In one way and another, therefore, by the 1890s Sir Joseph's own financial position was not healthy under the prosperous surface, and the bank was facing quite serious problems of liquidity. This was additionally dangerous in that it threatened the ability of the partners to meet their obligations to the public companies – the North Eastern Railway, the Consett Iron Company, and the Weardale and Shildon Water Company – which did a substantial part of their local banking business with J. and J. W. Pease. After the deaths of Gurney and Charles Pease in 1872 and 1873 had taken resources out of the bank the remaining partners, Sir Joseph and his brothers Edward and Arthur, knowing how serious it would be for the financing of the businesses and for the income of other relatives if any more portions had to be bought, provided in their wills that survivors should have the power to keep their business interests intact. Thus when Edward died in 1880 only his interest in the bank was bought out: his industrial assets were left in trust for his daughter Beatrice. The partners in the bank were now Sir Joseph with a 70% share, Arthur with 25%, and Alfred with 5%. When Jack came of age he too was made a partner with a 5% share transferred from his father.

To meet his and the bank's difficulties Sir Joseph sold property, including his first houses in London, and mortgaged the Hutton and Pinchinthorpe estates. He tried to cut personal expenditure without jeopardising his lifestyle, and borrowed from other banks on the security of his industrial assets. From 1893 the bank borrowed from other banks to enable it to pay the half-yearly dividends of the North Eastern Railway, the Consett Iron Company, and the Weardale and Shildon Water Company. Finally between 1898 and 1901 Henry Pease and Co. was reconstituted under new management and began to make modest profits: Arthur having died in 1898, Sir Joseph was the sole surviving partner. Robert Stephenson and Co. was reorganised as a public company: Sir Joseph sacrificed his claim to the debenture stock. Wilsons, Pease and Co. was also turned into a public company under new management.[62]

It is difficult to avoid the conclusion that it would have been better for Sir Joseph and his sons if these steps had been taken fifteen to twenty years earlier, and that a more dedicated businessman would have done so. It might also have been better for the companies and their employees: injecting more money without modernising plant and management did little to secure their future. It would certainly have been very difficult to close Henry Pease and Co., as Alfred wished to do. Not only was it the original family business; of greater practical importance was the fact that it was a substantial employer in the middle of Darlington, employing some 800 people; and Darlington was the base of all the Pease influence. Closure would have done a great deal of

---

[62] Kirby, *Men of Business*, pp. 81–3. The woollen business was eventually sold in 1920 to a Bradford company.

damage to the town and hence to the family's social and political standing. The decision in 1882 to keep the mills going on a limited basis secured existing jobs and did not obviate a possible later sale; but it did nothing to encourage energetic management. It might also have been difficult to dispose of Robert Stephenson and Co. and Wilsons Pease, but selling at a loss might have been better than allowing losses to accumulate.

There seem to be several reasons why hard decisions were not taken earlier. The Peases felt a strong sense of responsibility for their employees in bad times as well as good, and were generous, for example, with assistance for families of miners during strikes. Sir Joseph's diaries are full of anxieties about the affairs of the enterprises; but his political and social activities did not allow enough time for the kind of concentration on business that the problem areas required. After the debacle Henry Kitching, a Darlington iron manufacturer and fellow Quaker, reflected on the causes. The root of the trouble, he thought, might have been the distractions of political life and its social concomitants. Kitching doubted whether Alfred or Jack had ever done a hard day's work, and whether Sir Joseph paid much attention to his business affairs. Sir Joseph, as Kitching knew him, was optimistic and kind-hearted, generous to a degree, and full of unbounded belief in himself and his family. He had been brought up in an atmosphere where it was easy to borrow capital, so that a few thousand pounds more or less were of no consequence. The ease with which in the past the family had been able to borrow to build up the business encouraged them to see borrowing as the answer to every problem.[63]

Kitching did not accuse Sir Joseph of recklessness but rather of complacency and lack of attention to business. There had been a time in the 1840s when Joseph Pease could have been charged with imprudence in over-extending the family's commitments. But that crisis had been weathered; and Sir Joseph's optimism about commercial recovery was justified. The economy did pick up markedly in the late 1890s; but recovery came too late to save his credit and that of J. and J. W. Pease. Ironically, the final reorganisation of Pease and Partners and the upturn in coal prices in 1900 precipitated disaster.

The background was a long-running family problem. Beatrice Pease, Edward's daughter, owned a large block of shares in Pease and Partners, and smaller amounts in the Middlesbrough Estate and Robert Stephenson and Co. This substantial fortune was held in trust for her by Sir Joseph and Arthur Pease, until she was 21 or married under that age. In 1885, when she was nineteen, Beatrice married Newton Wallop, Viscount Lymington, a Cambridge acquaintance of Jack Pease and heir to the earldom of Portsmouth, to which he succeeded in 1891. The Portsmouths were not very wealthy, and

---

[63]   Notebook of Henry Kitching, c.1914, DCRO, D/Ki/303.

there is little doubt that Lymington was on the lookout for a rich wife. The couple's recurrent demands for money came at a time when Pease and Partners dividends were poor and in some years non-existent; and in 1893 Beatrice started a campaign to have the trust estate realised so that the proceeds could be reinvested in something more immediately rewarding.

Sir Joseph's position, from which he never departed in the next five years, was that in the present state of trade it would be foolish to try to sell the mining shares: they would only fetch about half their nominal value, so that there would be that much less to reinvest and future hopes of better dividends would be sacrificed. Beatrice's solicitor argued, equally consistently, that if the intrinsic value of the shares was so great, buyers could be found in a syndicate or in members and friends of the Pease family. This was the unspoken nub of the problem. In the current state of the coal trade the only potential purchasers at a reasonable price were the partners in the business, in effect Sir Joseph and his sons and Arthur, since other family members held only insignificant numbers of share and Sir David Dale held 10%. In the current state of J. and J. W. Pease and of the loss-making businesses Sir Joseph could hardly afford to buy his niece's shares; but eventually in March 1898, after the Portsmouths had threatened to take the trustees to court, a settlement was reached. It provided for the purchase, by Sir Joseph, Arthur, Alfred and Jack, of all the commercial assets of Edward Pease's estate. The price of the Pease and Partners shares was put at 67% of face value, and of those in Robert Stephenson at nil. The total sum involved was £273,000, of which four-fifths was to be paid at once.[64]

This was a large sum for the partners to produce, and they were obliged to consider 'rearranging' the capital of Pease and Partners. In May 1898 it was agreed that one way of doing so would be to float Pease and Partners as a public company. It was one thing for J. and J. W. Pease to arrange short-term accommodation from other banks to meet half-yearly obligations to the North Eastern Railway, the Consett Iron Company and the Weardale and Shildon Water Company, and Sir Joseph had no difficulty in doing so. To borrow money to pay out to the Portsmouths was another matter. British banks had virtually given up long-term investment in industry, but on the other hand the climate for public flotations was good. The prospectus for the new company was issued in September 1898, two months after the settlement with the Portsmouths had been confirmed in the High Court, and a month after Arthur Pease's death. Up to the last minute Sir Joseph was worried about taking this step, but the flotation was a great success: the ordinary shares were oversubscribed eight times over, the debentures twelve times. But the relief was short lived; for within a few weeks the Portsmouths announced their intention of applying to the High Court to have the settlement set aside.

[64]   Kirby, *Men of Business*, pp. 90–5, gives a full account of the whole affair.

The case was heard in the last weeks of 1900. The Portsmouths' case was that the trustees had not made a full disclosure of facts. The 33% discount on the Pease and Partners shares had been represented as giving a fair and reasonable price and as the only way to avoid a forced sale at an even lower price. But at the same time the trustees had been receiving expert advice that a public flotation could be launched successfully and yield a more than par price for the shares on offer. Against this it could be said that at the time of the settlement the flotation plan was still tentative – it was not finalised until four days before the actual date; that the Portsmouths, in their determination to force a conclusion, had stated their willingness to accept a settlement regardless of whether the shares might increase in value later; and that the flotation was forced on Sir Joseph by the necessity of paying the Portsmouths and would not have taken place otherwise. All this was true. Nevertheless the judge was pretty well bound to find that the trustees ought to have revealed that they were considering a public flotation.

Worse, for Sir Joseph's reputation, were the judge's strictures on his reliability as a witness as to the value of the private company. Its profits had been rising since 1896, and the price received for the shares on the public flotation bore little relation to his estimates of two years earlier. It was an extraordinary piece of chance that in the weeks before the flotation the price of coal was rising faster than at any time since 1874, filling potential investors with optimism. From Sir Joseph's point of view the timing could not have been worse. The agreement of 1898 was set aside. As a result the Pease family had to transfer to the Portsmouths a further block of shares in the new company valued at £241,000, make a cash payment of £61,000, and pay the Portsmouths' legal costs. In its new form Pease and Partners made gross profits of over £700,000 in the years 1899–1901, and declared dividends of 17½% and 20%. In so far as these dividends went to others, both the Portsmouths and the Pease family, who between them had owned 90% of the shares in the private company, paid, in profits foregone, a high price for the litigation.

The judge's decision was inevitably greatly coloured by the recent success of the coal trade. Alfred and Jack Pease were left feeling robbed, a natural reaction of two men who had been only marginally involved but were now landed with the price. Sir Joseph, whose integrity had been called in question and whose reputation was terribly damaged, was left above all feeling betrayed by his niece. Having provided her with a home until her marriage, having done all he could for her property in the bad times of the coal trade, having bought her shares under threat of legal action, having sold his and Arthur's mining property to pay for hers, then to be accused of fraud and, a boom having come on in coal prices, having to sacrifice still more of his own and Arthur's estates to pay her still more, was not just robbery but a cruel betrayal.[65] The Peases did not appeal against the judgment: they were advised that the most that could be hoped for was a removal of the imputation of dishonesty. That imputation therefore remained, but it was grossly unjust. What seems to have actuated Sir Joseph throughout was a patriarchal feeling of responsibility for the whole family, including Beatrice, and its collective property. Over the years of argument with the Portsmouths this personal feeling that he was responsible may have led Sir Joseph to be too dismissive of their importunities and may thus have fuelled their determination; but a fraudulent irresponsible trustee he was not.

The business world was marked in the 1890s by a movement towards mergers and amalgamations. In banking large joint stock companies absorbed smaller ones and a number of private banks. The merger activity reached a high point in 1896 with the foundation of Barclays Bank, which was to become one of the 'Big Five' after the First World War. Barclays was an amalgamation of three old-established Quaker private banks, Gurneys of Norwich, Backhouses of Darlington, and Barclays of London, together with a number of smaller ones. In view of the close connection between the Gurney, Backhouse and Pease families, it was natural that in 1898 Barclays should suggest taking over J. and J. W. Pease. Such a merger would give Barclays further important connections with North East business, especially the North Eastern Railway as well as Pease and Partners. Sir Joseph was too preoccupied with the Portsmouth affair and the public flotation to respond very quickly. But in the spring of 1902 the suggestion was renewed, and under pressure from his sons and Sir David Dale Sir Joseph agreed to negotiations for an amalgamation, and these began in the summer.[66] The only partners in the bank now were Sir Joseph and his two sons: when Arthur Pease died in 1898 his sons chose not to take on his share.

To begin with the negotiations proceeded on friendly and personal lines. Difficulties began when the Barclays negotiators raised the question of the security for the loan needed to cover the dividend payments of the North Eastern Railway and the Consett Iron Company, due in the last week of August. They were evidently worried about the extent of J. and J. W. Pease's liabilities, and asked that the partners should pledge the whole of their private estates as additional security. A preliminary agreement was reached on 19 August, between Alfred Pease and Henry Birkbeck, a friend of Sir Joseph's who was representing the London board of Barclays, under which Barclays would take over the whole of J. and J. W. Pease's business and Birkbeck would work out a scheme to put Sir Joseph's affairs on a sounder footing. Sir Joseph and his sons then went on holiday, only to be called back with the news that an eminent chartered accountant brought in by Barclays had discovered a clause in the articles of association of the Owners of the

[65]   J. W. Pease diary, 31 Dec. 1901, J. G. Pease Papers.
[66]   Kirby, *Men of Business*, pp. 101–10, is a full account; Joseph Sykes, *The Amalgamation Movement in English Banking 1825–1924*, London 1925, pp. 47–62.

Middlesbrough Estate giving them first claim on the shares of any person in debt to them. Sir Joseph was in debt to the Middlesbrough Owners, and the accountant advised Barclays to reject the entire arrangement, giving it as his opinion that J. and J. W. Pease was insolvent. The North Eastern Railway dividends were due on 23 August, and there was no time to arrange any other accommodation that would enable them to be paid. The Peases had no option but to accept, on 22 August, a document according to which Barclays would buy the good will of J. and J. W. Pease and the bank's assets, which were to include the private estates of the partners. The proceeds would be used to pay J. and J. W. Pease's creditors.

These terms involved the possible loss of the partners' personal fortunes, but seemed likely to save their credit. But even this consolation was removed by a public announcement from Barclays on 26 August that they were taking over most of the current business of J. and J. W. Pease but not its liabilities. This was catastrophic for the Peases' credit and instantly undermined the value of their assets. The reason why Barclays took this step, which by reducing the value of the assets harmed also themselves and J. and J. W. Pease's creditors, does not seem to be recorded. In strict accountancy terms it may have been rational: in longer banking terms it did not make very good sense.

The partners were rescued from bankruptcy in the next few weeks by the creation of a guarantee fund subscribed by local friends, relatives and industrialists and even by individual members of Barclays' board. Finally in December 1902 an agreement was signed under which all the estates and effects of J. and J.W Pease, and the partners' private estates except for furniture and personal effects, were handed over to a private company. Its capital would be distributed among the creditors and Barclays would make a loan – in effect a mortgage – against the security of the disposable assets and the guarantee fund. These terms suited Barclays, and promised the major creditors at least as much as they would get from proceedings in bankruptcy. They avoided the embarrassment for a bank of Quaker origin and still substantial Quaker participation of forcing a man of Sir Joseph's standing into a bankruptcy that might cost him his membership of the Society of Friends. But Sir Joseph was not spared a number of other humiliations. He had to resign all his directorships and was treated with scant courtesy by the North Eastern Railway. He decided to retire from Parliament at the next general election. He had to leave Hutton Hall (which was eventually sold for not much more than half the 1902 valuation), and went to live at his Falmouth house, where he died of heart failure on 23 June 1903, his seventy-fifth birthday. Guisborough Monthly Meeting assured his son that the family had not forfeited the respect of the meeting, but mixed its sympathy with a certain disapproval of the way the bank's affairs had been supervised. Sir Joseph was given only a two-line obituary in the Quaker *Annual Monitor*, in contrast to his father's ten pages and his brother Arthur's six.[67]

Sir Joseph's sons paid a heavy price for their partnerships without power in J. and J.W Pease. After the collapse Alfred was left with nothing but his furniture and personal belongings. He resigned his seat in Parliament, and took a government post in South Africa where he spent the next five years. With help from relatives he was able to rescue Pinchinthorpe, and after the First World War and two more African ventures he settled for country life and its obligations such as membership of North Riding County Council. Alfred was sore at not being restored to the board of Pease and Partners, but he showed no disposition to work in the firm. He did return to the Middlesbrough Owners and became managing director. Jack suffered less. His London house was in his mother-in-law's name; he was able to rent, and before long to buy a house at Gainford on the Tees in place of Nunthorpe on which Sir Joseph had spent so much money. His wife used to describe Headlam Hall as 'our little Yorkshire shooting box,' despite the facts that the house was large and Gainford is on the north bank of the river: County Durham would have conjured up quite the wrong image.[68] Jack concentrated on politics, becoming Liberal chief whip under Asquith, Chancellor of the Duchy of Lancaster in 1910, President of the Board of Education a year later and finally Postmaster General in 1916. He left the government, with a peerage as Lord Gainford, when Lloyd George succeeded Asquith. Jack had been restored to the board of Pease and Partners in 1904, and when his political career came to an end he was able to take up a new one in coal. He represented the Mining Association of Great Britain before the Sankey Commission on the Coal Industry in 1919, and became deputy chairman of the Durham Coal Owners Association and vice chairman of the Durham Coke Owners. He represented a hard employers' line in the discussions of the 1920s on the future of the coal industry, but was rather more flexible and imaginative behind the scenes. He became chairman of Pease and Partners in 1927.

In this position Lord Gainford succeeded his cousin Arthur Francis Pease. Arthur's sons, having chosen not to take up their father's interest in J. and J. W. Pease, were spared the consequences of the bank's collapse, and two were active in Pease and Partners. Arthur Francis became chairman and managing director in 1906 on the death of Sir David Dale: he was also a director of the London and North Eastern Railway and active in County Durham affairs. Arthur Francis's son Richard became chairman of Pease and Partners when Lord Gainford died, and was chairman of a rump ironstone company after

---

[67] Society of Friends, *Annual Monitor*, 1904; Guisborough Monthly Meeting minute, May 1904; J. A. Pease to clerk of meeting, 3 Aug., Gainford Papers, 78.

[68] Pease, *Wealth of Happiness*, p. 332. For Jack's political career see Cameron Hazlehurst and Christine Woodland, eds., *A Liberal Chronicle. Journals and Papers of J. A. Pease, 1st Lord Gainford*, Vol. 1, London 1994.

coal nationalisation, until it was wound up in 1958. Descendants of Joseph Pease were therefore closely connected with the coal industry to the date of its nationalisation. Lord Gainford died in 1943. His only son Joseph qualified as a colliery manager but left the firm in 1931. None of Alfred's sons joined it. A grandson of John Beaumont Pease, William Edwin, continued the family's close connection with Darlington until the 1920s, living there, serving as mayor, representing the town in Parliament for three years, and sitting on the board of the Darlington-based Cleveland Bridge and Engineering Company as well as of the Consett Iron Company.

Whilst members of the Pease family remained active and even prominent in the affairs of North East England, the concentration of business, social and political influence did not last. The political influence was on the wane in south Durham by the time Sir Joseph died, and could hardly have continued with a mass electorate. After the First World War the Durham county constituencies became almost uniformly and almost permanently Labour seats. Darlington, Stockton and Hartlepool had Conservative and Liberal representatives in the 1920s. In Darlington the Pease name lasted until 1928, now attached to Conservatism; but since the town did not defy the general pattern of results it would be hard to say whether the name was worth any substantial number of votes: the majorities do not seem to reflect much personal attachment. Herbert Pike Pease represented the town from 1898 to 1923, with only a six-month break in 1910. When he was raised to the peerage he was succeeded by his cousin William Edwin; but when the latter died in 1928 his brother was defeated in the ensuing by-election. When Sir Joseph's grandson Joseph Gurney Pease stood for Darlington as a Liberal in 1964, he did not find that his name had any political resonance.[69]

The kind of social influence exercised by large employers survived in single-industry towns, but had more rivals after the First World War as local and national government took on more roles in housing and welfare provision. The business empire built up by Joseph Pease in the 1840s and 50s – the horizontal integration of coal, coke, iron, limestone and railways – had quite a short life. The amalgamation of the Stockton and Darlington Railway with the North Eastern Railway in 1863 was the first breach. Peases remained major shareholders in the North Eastern Railway; Henry and Sir Joseph served on the board; Sir Joseph was chairman from 1894 until 1903. But the management of railways no longer resembled or functioned in the same way as family businesses; they were now run by professional managers answerable to boards of powerful and wealthy directors. As an important local industrialist Sir Joseph sat on the North Eastern board along with others such as Sir David Dale, the ironmaster Sir Isaac Lowthian Bell and the coal owner Sir James Joicey, and representatives of shipbuilding, agriculture and politics.

[69]   Personal communication, J. Gurney Pease.

The practical difference was, however, perhaps not so great. The Stockton and Darlington Railway had not, for example, given preference to Pease-produced coal in its rates; the North Eastern Railway maintained a pricing policy that seems to have put the interests of the regional economy above those of long-run profits and the dividends of shareholders. The Quaker inheritance has been suggested as an explanation, but the public service outlook was more widely diffused.[70]

Becoming a public company did not make much difference to the way Pease and Partners was managed. In the following twenty years there were a number of amalgamations and flotations in the coal industry, but still after the First World War even the large and dominant firms continued to resemble private rather than public concerns, and remained the preserve of a small group or even a single family.[71] Survival of family managerial control after public flotation was not confined to the mining industry. The most important factors in such survival seem to have been the size of family share-holdings and the number of family members capable of leadership. After 1903 family shareholding in Pease and Partners was greatly reduced; and although several members of the family remained on the board until 1933 not all of them were very active. By that time the firm was no longer among the nine largest colliery companies and was suffering severely from the depression.

After the First World War Pease and Partners shared the vicissitudes of the coal industry, which was short of investment funds, hampered in any attempts at reorganisation by badly shaped royalties and dispersed ownership, and marked by conservatism on all sides. The company had once had a distinctive character derived from its owners' Quakerism. By 1918 few of the Peases were still Quakers, and paternalism had gone from the industrial scene. Whereas one can suppose that Joseph Pease and his sons would have supported the movement for pit-head baths, in 1919 Lord Gainford could doubt whether the miners really wanted them. After the 1926 strike and lockout Pease and Partners was not singled out by the union, as the Consett Iron Company was, for opprobrium for victimising strikers, but it shared the generally hard managerial stance, no longer, for example, allowing even a day's free coal or a week's lease of a house to a miner on his retirement.[72] The industrial environment had changed: the Peases had changed too.

[70] Irving, *North Eastern Railway*, pp. 129–32, 137–8.

[71] Barry Supple, *History of the British Coal Industry*, Vol. 4, Oxford 1982, p. 402.

[72] W. R. Garside, *The Durham Miners 1919-1960*, London 1971, pp. 231, 292, 295; Moore, *Pit-men, Preachers and Politics*, pp. 154–5. For the coal industry's structure and management see Supple, *Coal Industry*, Vol. 4, pp. 361–424, 616–17.

BIBLIOGRAPHY

Unpublished Sources

Consett
Consett Iron Company records.

Durham, County Record Office
Darlington Borough Council: minutes; Board of Health minutes.
Darlington Library Collection.
Darlington: Miscellaneous.
Darlington Poor Law Union: Board of Guardians minutes.
Hodgkin Collection.
Kitching Collection.
Londonderry Papers.
Mewburn Diaries.
National Coal Board records: Buddle Collection; Durham Coal Owners Association.
Pease Collection.
Gurney Pease Collection.
Pease-Stephenson Papers.
Society of Friends: Darlington Monthly Meeting; Darlington Preparative Meeting; Raby Monthly Meeting.
Strathmore Papers.

London, British Library
Gladstone Papers

London, Friends House
Religious Society of Friends archives.

London, House of Lords Record Office
House of Commons: Evidence, 1853, Vols. 72–3. Select Committee on Railway Bills, Darlington and Barnard Castle Railway.
Evidence, 1854, Vol. 44. Select Committee on Private Bills, Barnard Castle and Bishop Auckland Junction Railway and Branch Bill.

Evidence, 1854, Vol. 45. Select Committee on Private Bills, Darlington and Barnard Castle Railway.

Evidence, 1856, Vol. 34. Select Committee on Private Bills, Middlesbrough Extension and Improvement Bill.

Evidence, 1858, Vols. 18–19. Select Committee on Railway Bills. Durham and Cleveland Union Railway Bill.

Evidence, 1858, Vol. 48. Select Committee on Private Bills, Middlesbrough Improvement Bill.

Evidence, 1859, Vol. 12. Select Committee on Railway Bills, Cleveland Railway Bill.

House of Lords: Evidence, 1856. Minutes of Evidence taken before the Select Committee of the House of Lords on the Middlesbrough Improvement Act.

London, Public Record Office
Board of Trade: company registers BT 31.
Stockton and Darlington Railway records: RAIL 667.

Middlesbrough, Cleveland County Archives
British Steel Corporation archives.
Improvement Commission minutes.
Owners of the Middlesbrough Estate records.

Newcastle upon Tyne, City Library
South Durham Poll Book, 1857.
Tomlinson Collection.

Newcastle upon Tyne, Northumberland Record Office
Armstrong Collection.
Culley Papers.
Johnson Collection.
North East Institute of Mining Engineers, Watson Collection.

Newcastle upon Tyne, Tyne and Wear Archives
Wilson of Forest Hall Collection.

Oxford, Nuffield College
Gainford Papers.

Published Sources

Official Publications

General Board of Health. *Report to the General Board of Health on a Preliminary Inquiry into the Sewerage, Drainage, and Supply of Water, and the Sanitary Condition of the Inhabitants of the Township of Crook and Billy Row, in the County of Durham. By T. W. Rammell, Esq.* London 1854.

——. *Report to the General Board of Health on a Preliminary Inquiry into the Sewerage, Drainage, and Supply of Water, and the Sanitary Condition of the Inhabitants of the Town of Darlington, in the County of Durham. By William Ranger, Esq.* London 1850.

——. *Report to the General Board of Health on a Preliminary Inquiry into the Sewerage, Drainage and Supply of Water, and the Sanitary Condition of the Inhabitants of the Borough of Middlesbrough, in the North Riding of the County of York. By William Ranger, Esq.* London 1854.

House of Commons. *Commission for Inquiring into the Employment and Condition of Children in Mines and Manufactories. First Report of the Commissioners, and Appendixes.* Parliamentary Papers, 1842, Vols. 15, 16, 17.

——. *Report of the Admiralty, under Act 11 & 12 Vict., c. 129, Tees River Conservancy Bill.* Parliamentary Papers, 1851, Vol. 29.

——. *Report of the Commissioner appointed, under the Provisions of the Act 5 & 6 Vict., c. 99, to Inquire into the Operation of that Act, and into the State of the Population in the Mining Districts, 1846.* Parliamentary Papers, 1846, Vol. 24.

——. *Report of the Commissioner appointed, under the Provisions of the Act 5 & 6 Vict., c. 99. to Inquire into the Operation of that Act, and into the State of the Population of the Mining Districts, 1853.* Parliamentary Papers, 1852–3, Vol. 40.

——. *Report of the Commissioner appointed, under the Provisions of the Act 5 & 6 Vict., c. 99, to Inquire into the Operation of that Act, and into the State of the Population of the Mining Districts, 1858.* Parliamentary Papers, 1858, Vol. 32.

——. *Report of the Commissioner appointed, under the Provisions of the Act 5 & 6 Vict., c. 99, to Inquire into the Operation of that Act, and into the State of the Population of the Mining Districts, 1859.* Parliamentary Papers, 1859, sess. 2, Vol. 12.

——. *Report of the Commissioners appointed to Inquire into the Condition of all Mines in Great Britain to which the Provisions of the Act 23 & 24 Vict., c. 151, do not apply.* Parliamentary Papers, 1864, Vol. 24.

——. *Report from the Select Committee on Coal, together with the Proceedings of the Committee, Minutes of Evidence, and Appendix.* Parliamentary Papers, 1873, Vol. 10.

——. *Report from the Select Committee on Education of the Poorer Classes in England and Wales, together with Minutes of Evidence.* Parliamentary Papers, 1837–8, Vol. 7.

House of Lords. *Select Committee on the Coal Trade.* Sessional Papers, 1829, Vol. 8.

The Parliamentary Debates. 3rd series, 4th series.

Privy Council. *Report of the Commissioners appointed to Inquire into the State of Popular Education in England.* 6 vols. London 1861.

Theses

Emery, Norman. 'Pease and Partners and the Deerness Valley.' MA, University of Durham, 1984.

Leonard, J. W. 'Urban Development and Population Growth in Middlesbrough 1831–1871.' PhD, University of York 1976.

Rennison, R. W. 'The Development of the North Eastern Coal Ports 1815–1914.' PhD, University of Newcastle upon Tyne 1987.

Seeley, J. Y. E. 'Coal Mining Villages of Northumberland and Durham. A Study of Sanitary Conditions and Social Facilities 1870–1889.' MA, University of Newcastle upon Tyne 1973.

Wilson, Arthur Struthers. 'The Consett Iron Company Ltd., a Case Study in Victorian Business History.' M.Phil, University of Durham 1973.

Newspapers and Periodicals

Darlington Mercury
Darlington and Richmond Herald
Darlington and Stockton Mercury
Darlington and Stockton Telegraph
Darlington and Stockton Times
Darlington Telegraph
Durham Chronicle
Durham County Advertiser
The Friend
Friends Quarterly Examiner
Newcastle Courant
Newcastle Daily Express
Newcastle Weekly Chronicle
Northern Echo
South Durham and Cleveland Mercury
South Durham Herald

BIBLIOGRAPHY

Books and Articles cited

Alderman, Geoffrey. *The Railway Interest*. Leicester 1973.

Allott, Stephen. *Friends in York. The Quaker Story in the Life of a Meeting*. York 1978.

Bailey, John. *General View of the Agriculture in the County of Durham, with Observations on the Means of its Improvement. Drawn up for the Consideration of the Board of Agriculture and Internal Improvement*. London 1810.

Bell, Florence. *At the Works. A Study of a Manufacturing Town*. London 1907.

Benson, John. *British Coalminers in the Nineteenth Century. A Social History*. Dublin 1980.

Birch, Alan. *The Economic History of the British Iron and Steel Industry 1784–1879*. London 1967.

Boyce, Ann Ogden. *Records of a Quaker family. The Richardsons of Cleveland*. London 1889.

Boyson, Rhodes. *The Ashworth Cotton Enterprise. The Rise and Fall of a Family Firm 1818–1880*. Oxford 1970.

Braithwaite, William C. *The Second Period of Quakerism*. 2nd edn. Cambridge 1961.

Brown, H. Diana. 'Colliery Cottages 1830–1915. The Great Northern Coalfield.' *Archaeologia Aeliana*, 5th ser. 23 (1995), pp. 291–305.

Carr, J. C., and Taplin, W. *History of the British Steel Industry*. Oxford 1962.

Chapman, Vera. *Rural Darlington. Farm, Mansion and Suburb*. Durham 1975.

Church, Roy. *The History of the British Coal Industry*. Vol. 3, *1830–1913*. Oxford 1986.

Coleman, D. C. *Courtaulds. An Economic and Social History*. 3 vols. Oxford 1969–80.

Colls, Robert. '"Oh Happy English Children!" Coal, class and education in the North East.' *Past and Present*, 73 (1976), pp. 75–99.

Corley, T. A. B. *Quaker Enterprise in Biscuits. Huntley and Palmers of Reading 1872–1972*. London 1972.

Craig, F. W. S. *British Electoral Facts 1832–1987*. 5th edn. Aldershot 1989.

Dale, Sir David. *Thirty Years Experience of Industrial Conciliation and Arbitration*. London 1899.

Davies, Hunter. *George Stephenson: a Biographical Study of the Father of the Railways*. London 1975.

The Electors' Scrap Book. Durham 1832.

Ellens, J. P. *Religious Routes to Gladstonian Liberalism: the Church Rate Conflict in England and Wales, 1832–1868*. University Park, PA 1994.

Emery, Norman. *The Deerness Valley. The History of a Settlement in a Durham Valley*. Durham 1988.

Farnie, D. A. *John Rylands of Manchester*. Manchester 1993.

Ferguson, John, ed. *Christianity, Society and Education*. London 1981.

Fitzgerald, Robert. *Rowntree and the Marketing Revolution, 1862–1969.* Cambridge 1995.

Flinn, Michael W. *The History of the British Coal Industry.* Vol. 2, *1700–1830.* Oxford 1984.

Fordyce, William. *The History and Antiquities of the County Palatine of Durham.* 2 vols. Newcastle upon Tyne 1857.

——. *A History of Coal, Coke, Coal Fields, Coal Mines, Iron, its Ores, and Processes of Manufacture.* Newcastle upon Tyne 1860.

Fortunes Made in Business. A Series of Original Sketches, Biographical and Anecdotal, from the Recent History of Industry and Commerce, by Various Writers. Vol. 1. London 1884.

Foster, Joseph. *Pease of Darlington.* N.p. 1891.

Friends, Religious Society of. *Annual Monitor; or Obituary of the Members of the Society of Friends in Great Britain and Ireland.* York and London 1842ff.

——. *Epistles from the Yearly Meeting of Friends, held in London, to the Quarterly and Monthly Meetings in Great Britain, Ireland, and Elsewhere; from 1681 to 1857 inclusive.* 2 vols. London 1858.

——. *Extracts from the Minutes and Epistles of the Yearly Meeting of the Religious Society of Friends, held in London from its First Institution to the Present Time, relating to Christian Doctrine, Practice and Discipline.* 4th edn. London 1861; 5th edn. London 1871.

——. *Yearly Meeting Proceedings.* London 1859 ff.

Fynes, Richard. *The History of the Northumberland and Durham Miners.* Sunderland 1873.

Galloway, Robert. *Annals of Coal Mining and the Coal Trade.* 2 vols. London 1898, 1904.

Gardiner, A. G. *Life of George Cadbury.* London 1923.

Garside, W. R. *The Durham Miners 1919–1960.* London 1971.

[Grant, James]. *Random Recollections of the House of Commons, from the Year 1830 to the Close of 1835 ... By One of No Party.* London 1836.

Gregory, Roy. *The Miners and British Politics 1906–1914.* Oxford 1968.

Grey, Sir Edward. *Sir David Dale. Inaugural Address delivered for the Dale Memorial Trust, to which is prefaced a Memoir by Howard Pease.* London 1911.

Gurney, Joseph John. *The Memoirs of Joseph John Gurney,* ed. Joseph Bevan Braithwaite. 2 vols. Norwich 1854.

Hair, T. H. *A Series of Views of the Collieries in the Counties of Northumberland and Durham.* London 1844.

Halloway, Ena L., and Hughes, Alan. *New Marske Looking Back.* New Marske 1982.

Hamilton, Mary Agnes. *Arthur Henderson.* London 1938.

Harrison, Brian. *Drink and the Victorians. The Temperance Question in England 1815–1872.* London 1971.

BIBLIOGRAPHY

Harte, Negley, and Quincault, Roland, eds. *Land and Society in Britain 1700–1914. Essays in Honour of F. M. L. Thompson*. Manchester 1996.

Hazlehurst, Cameron, and Woodland, Christine, eds. *A Liberal Chronicle. Journals and Papers of J. A. Pease, 1st Lord Gainford*. Vol. 1, London 1994.

Heesom, A. J. 'Entrepreneurial Paternalism. The Third Lord Londonderry (1778–1854) and the Coal Trade.' *Durham University Journal*, 66 (1974), pp. 238–56.

Heesom, A. J., and Duffy, Brendan. 'Debate. Coal, Class and Education in the North East.' *Past and Present*. 90 (1981), pp. 136–51.

Hempstead, C. A., ed. *Cleveland Iron and Steel. Background and Nineteenth Century History*. Redcar 1979.

History of the Darlington and Barnard Castle Railway, with Notices of the Stockton and Darlington, Clarence, West Hartlepool and other Railways and Companies in the District by an Inhabitant of Barnard Castle [Thompson Richardson]. London 1877.

The History of the British Coal Industry. Vol. 2, *1700–1830*, by Michael W. Flinn, Oxford 1984; Vol. 3, *1830–1913*, by Roy Church, Oxford 1986; Vol. 4, *1913–1946*, by Barry Supple, Oxford 1987.

Holland, John. *The History and Description of Fossil Fuel, the Collieries and Coal Trade of Great Britain*. London 1835.

Irving, R. J. *The North Eastern Railway Company 1870–1914. An Economic History*. Leicester 1976.

Isichei, Elizabeth. *Victorian Quakers*. Oxford 1970.

Jeans, J. S. *Jubilee Memorial of the Railway System. A History of the Stockton and Darlington Railway and a Record of its Results*. London 1875.

——. *Pioneers of the Cleveland Iron Trade*. Middlesbrough 1875.

Jeremy, David J., ed. *Business and Religion in Britain*. Aldershot 1988.

——. *Religion, Business and Wealth in Modern Britain*. London and New York 1998.

——, and Shaw, Christine, eds. *Dictionary of Business Biography*. 6 vols. London 1984–6.

Jolly, W. P. *Lord Leverhulme. A Biography*. London 1976.

Kelly's Directory of Durham. London 1879.

The Kings of British Commerce. The Peases of the North of England. Founders of the First Railway in the World. N.p., n.d. [1876].

Kirby, M. W. *Men of Business and Politics. The Rise and Fall of the Quaker Pease Dynasty of North-East England, 1700–1943*. London 1984.

——. *The Origins of Railway Enterprise: Stockton and Darlington Railway, 1821*. Cambridge 1993.

Lee, Alan J. *The Origins of the Popular Press in England 1855–1914*. London 1976.

Leifchild, J. R. *Our Coal and Our Coal Pits. The People in them and the Scenes around them. By a Traveller Underground*. London 1853.

Leventhal, F. M. *Arthur Henderson*. London 1989.

Lillie, William. *The History of Middlesbrough. An Illustration of the Evolution of English Industry*. Middlesbrough 1968.

Lloyd, Edward. *The Story of Fifty years of Crook Cooperative Society*. Pelaw 1916.

Longstaffe, W. Hylton Dyer. *The History and Antiquities of the Parish of Darlington in the Bishoprick*. Darlington and London 1854.

Machin, G. I. T. *Politics and the Churches in Great Britain 1832 to 1868*. Oxford 1977.

Mackenzie, Aeneas, and Ross, Metcalf. *An Historical, Topographical and Descriptive View of the County Palatine of Durham*. Newcastle upon Tyne 1834.

Marriner, Sheila. *Rathbones of Liverpool 1845–73*. Liverpool 1861.

Martin, Major R. *Historical Notes and Personal Recollections of West Hartlepool and Its Founder, with Chronological Notes*. West Hartlepool 1924.

Metcalf, G. H. *A History of the Durham Miners Association 1869–1915*. Durham 1947.

Mewburn, Francis. *The Larchfield Diary. Extracts from the Diary of the late Mr Mewburn, First Railway Solicitor*. Darlington 1866.

Mewburn Francis Jr. *Memoir of Fra: Mewburn, Chief Bailiff of Darlington and First Railway Solicitor, by his Son*. Darlington 1867.

Milne, Maurice. *The Newspapers of Northumberland and Durham. A Study of their Progress during the 'Golden Age' of the Provincial Press*. Newcastle upon Tyne [1971].

Moore, D. C. *The Politics of Deference. A Study of the Mid-Nineteenth Century English Political System*. Hassocks 1976.

Moore, Robert. *Pit-Men, Preachers and Politics. The Effects of Methodism in a Durham Mining Community*. Cambridge 1974.

Moorsom, Norman. *The Book of Middlesbrough*. Buckingham 1986.

——, ed. *The Stockton and Darlington Railway. The Foundation of Middlesbrough*. Middlesbrough 1975.

Musson, A. E. *Enterprise in Soap and Chemicals. Joseph Crosfield and Sons Ltd. 1815–1965*. Manchester 1965.

Northern Echo. *The Durham Thirteen. Biographical Sketches of the Members of Parliament returned from the City, Boroughs and County of Durham at the General Election of 1874*. Darlington 1874.

Nossiter, T. J. *Influence, Opinion and Political Idioms in Reformed England. Case Studies from the North East 1832–74*. Hassocks 1975.

Ord, John Walker. *The History and Antiquities of Cleveland. Comprising the Wapentake of East and West Langbargh, North Riding, County York*. London 1846. New edn, Stockton-on-Tees, 1972.

Orme, Eliza. *Lady Fry of Darlington*. London 1898.

Pallister, Ray. 'Educational investment by industrialists in the early part of the nineteenth century in County Durham.' *Durham University Journal*, 61 (1968-9), pp. 32-8.

Peacock, A. J. *George Hudson 1800-1871. The Railway King*. 2 vols. York 1988-9.

Pease, Sir Alfred, ed. *The Diaries of Edward Pease, the Father of English Railways*. London 1907.

P., E. F. [Elizabeth Fell Pease]. *Thoughts in Quiet Hours*. London 1890.

Pease, Henry, and Co. *Bi-centenary 1752-1952. Priestgate Mills, Darlington*. Darlington 1952.

Pease, Joseph Gurney. ed., *A Wealth of Happiness and Many Bitter Trials. The Journals of Sir Alfred Pease, a Restless Man*. York 1992.

Pease, Mary H. *Henry Pease. A Short Story of his Life*. London 1897.

Phillips, Maberley. *A History of Banks, Bankers and Banking in Northumberland, Durham and North Yorkshire*. London 1894.

Pollard, A. J., ed. *Middlesbrough. Town and Community*. Stroud 1996.

Pratt, David H. *English Quakers and the First Industrial Revolution. A Study of the Quaker Communities in Four Industrial Counties – Lancashire, Yorkshire, Warwick and Gloucester 1750-1830*. New York and London 1985.

Pressnell, L. S. *Country Banking in the Industrial Revolution*. Oxford 1956.

Purdue, A. W. 'Arthur Henderson and Liberal, Liberal Labour and Labour Politics in the North East of England 1892-1905.' *Northern History*, 11(1975), pp. 195-217.

Random Recollections of the House of Commons, from the Year 1830 to the Close of 1835 ... By One of No Party [James Grant]. London 1836.

Reed, M. C. *Investment in Railways in Britain 1820-1844. A Study in the Development of the Capital Market*. London 1975.

Reid, H. G., ed. *Middlesbrough and its Jubilee*. Middlesbrough 1881.

Richardson, George. *The Annals of the Cleveland Richardsons and their Descendants, Compiled from Family Manuscripts*. Newcastle upon Tyne 1850.

Richardson. M. A. *The Local Historian's Table Book of Remarkable Occurrences, Historical Facts, Traditions, Legendary and Descriptive Ballads, etc., etc., Connected with the Counties of Newcastle upon Tyne, Northumberland and Durham. Historical Division*. 6 vols. London 1841-6.

[Richardson, Thompson]. *History of the Darlington and Barnard Castle Railway, with Notices of the Stockton and Darlington, Clarence, West Hartlepool and other Railways and Companies in the District, by an Inhabitant of Barnard Castle*. London 1877.

Ross, Thomas, and Stoddart, Andrew. *Jubilee History of the Annfield Plain Cooperative Society Ltd. 1870 to 1920*. Manchester 1921.

Rounthwaite, T. E. *The Railways of Weardale*. London 1965.

Rowntree, John Stephenson. *Quakerism, Past and Present: being an Inquiry into the Causes of its Decline in Great Britain and Ireland.* London 1859.

Rubinstein, W. D. 'Businessmen into landowners: the Question Revisited.' in *Land and Society in Britain, 1700–1914. Essays in Honour of F. M. L. Thompson,* ed. Negley Harte and Roland Quincault. Manchester 1996.

——. *Elites and the Wealthy in Modern British History.* Brighton 1987.

——. *Men of Property. The Very Wealthy in Britain since the Industrial Revolution.* London 1981.

Sansbury, Ruth. *Beyond the Blew Stone. 300 Years of Quakers in Newcastle.* Newcastle upon Tyne 1998.

Sharp, Sir Cuthbert. *History of Hartlepool, being a Reprint of the Original Work Published in 1816, with a Supplemental History, to 1851, Inclusive.* Hartlepool 1851.

Smith, H. John, ed. *Public Health Act. Report to the General Board of Health on Darlington 1850.* Durham 1967.

Spencer, Henry. *Men that are Gone from the Households of Darlington.* Darlington and London 1862.

Steel, John William. *'Friendly Sketches.' Essays illustrative of Quakerism.* London and Darlington 1876.

——. *A Historical Sketch of the Society of Friends in Newcastle and Gateshead 1653–1898.* Newcastle upon Tyne 1899.

Stoddart, Anna M. *Saintly Lives. Elizabeth Pease Nichol.* London 1899.

Sturge, Joseph. *Some Account of a Deputation from the ... Society of Friends to the Emperor of Russia.* London 1854.

Surtees, Robert. *History and Antiquities of the County Palatine of Durham.* 4 vols. London 1816–40.

Supple, Barry. *The History of the British Coal Industry.* Vol. 4, *1913–1946.* Oxford 1987.

Sutton, George Barry. *C. & J. Clark 1833–1903. A History of Shoemaking in Street, Somerset.* York 1979.

Swift, David E. *Joseph John Gurney. Banker, Reformer and Quaker.* Middletown, CT 1962.

Sykes, John. *Local Records; or Historical Register of Remarkable Events, which have Occurred in Northumberland and Durham, Newcastle upon Tyne and Berwick upon Tweed, from the Earliest Period of Authentic Record, to the Present Time; with Biographical Notices of Deceased Persons of Talent, Eccentricity, and Longevity.* New edn. 2 vols. Newcastle upon Tyne 1833.

Sykes, Joseph. *The Amalgamation Movement in English Banking 1825–1924.* London 1925.

Tate, William. *A Description of these Highly Noted Watering Places in the County of Durham, Hartlepool and Seaton Carew.* 2nd edn., Stockton 1816.

Tomlinson, William Weaver. *The North Eastern Railway: its Rise and Development.* Newcastle upon Tyne 1915.

Trevelyan, G. M. *The Life of John Bright*. London 1913.

Vann, Richard T. *Social Development of English Quakerism*. Cambridge, MA 1969.

Vernon, Anne. *A Quaker Business Man. The Life of Joseph Rowntree 1836–1935*. York 1982.

Waggott, Eric. *Jackson's Town. The Story of the Creation of West Hartlepool and the Success and Downfall of its Founder, Ralph Ward Jackson*. Hartlepool 1980.

Walvin, James. *The Quakers. Money and Morals*. London 1997.

Ward, W. R. *Religion and Society in England 1790–1850*. London 1972.

Watts, Michael R. *The Dissenters*. 2 vols. Oxford 1978, 1995.

Welbourne, E. *Miners' Unions of Northumberland and Durham*. Cambridge 1923.

Wesley, John. *Works*. Bicentennial edn. *Journal and Diaries*, ed. W. R. Ward and Richard P. Heitzenrater. 6 vols. *Sermons*, ed. A. C. Outler. 4 vols. Nashville 1982ff.

White, J. W., and Simpson, R. *Jubilee History of the West Stanley Cooperative Society Ltd. 1876 to 1926*. Pelaw 1926.

Williams, Iolo A. *The Firm of Cadbury 1831–1931*. London 1931.

Wilson, John. *History of the Durham Miners Association 1870–1904*. Durham 1907.

Wilson, Thomas. *The Pitman's Pay, and other Poems*. Gateshead 1843.

Windsor, David Burns. *The Quaker Enterprise. Friends in Business*. London 1980.

Wood, Robert. *West Hartlepool. The Rise and Development of a Victorian New Town*. West Hartlepool 1967.

Wright, Sheila. *Friends in York. The Dynamics of Quaker Revival 1780–1860*. Keele 1995.

Wrigley, Chris. *Arthur Henderson*. Cardiff 1990.

INDEX

INDEX

1. Edward Pease, 1767–1858; W. Miller after an unknown artist.
By courtesy of the National Portrait Gallery.

2. Edward Pease as an old man, 1848.
By courtesy of Darlington Library and Art Gallery.

3. Joseph Pease as a young man.
By courtesy of Darlington Library and Art Gallery.

4. Joseph Pease, oils, painted by H. J. Wright in 1874.
By courtesy of the National Railway Museum, Science and Society Picture library.

5. Henry Pease, lithograph of *c.*1875.
By courtesy of the National Railway Museum, Science and Society library.

6. Joseph Whitwell Pease.
By courtesy of Darlington Library and Art Gallery.

7. Sir Joseph Whitwell Pease, photograph of *c*.1896.
By kind permission of J. Gurney Pease.

8. John Dobbin, opening of the Stockton and Darlington Railway. *Watercolour by courtesy of Darlington Borough Art Collection.*

9. Premises of the Friends' Meeting House in Darlington in 1838. *By courtesy of Darlington Library and Art Gallery.*

10. Hutton Hall, watercolour sketch of c.1876. *By courtesy of Darlington Library and Art Gallery.*

11. St Helen Auckland Colliery. 1844. From T. H. Hair, *A Series of Views of the Colleries in the Counties of Northumberland and Durham.*
By courtesy of Durham University Library.

14. The first house built in Middlesbrough. *By courtesy of Teesside Archives.*

12 (opposite, top). Middlesbrough in 1832. *By courtesy of Middlesbrough Central Library.*

13 (opposite, below). Middlesbrough South St in 1855. *By courtesy of Middlesbrough Central Library.*

15. Crook British Schools, 1866; *author's photograph.*

16. Colliery housing at Esh Winning, *author's photograph.*

17. Colliery housing at Esh Winning, photographed by H. Abrams in 1972–3.
By courtesy of Durham Record Office.

18. Statue of Joseph Pease, unveiled in 1875.
By courtesy of Darlington Library and Art Gallery.